THE INSTITUTE FOR MEDICAL
LEADERSHIP

With best wishes for lasting success,

Susan F. Reynolds, MD, PhD

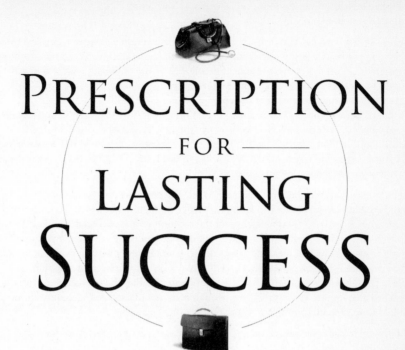

# PRESCRIPTION
## — FOR —
# LASTING
# SUCCESS

**LEADERSHIP STRATEGIES
TO DIAGNOSE PROBLEMS AND
TRANSFORM YOUR ORGANIZATION**

## SUSAN F. REYNOLDS, MD, PHD

WILEY

JOHN WILEY & SONS, INC.

Published by John Wiley & Sons, Inc., Hoboken, New Jersey.
Published simultaneously in Canada.

For general information on our other products and services or for technical support, please contact our Customer Care Department within the United States at (800) 762-2974, outside the United States at (317) 572-3993 or fax (317) 572-4002.

Wiley publishes in a variety of print and electronic formats and by print-on-demand. Some material included with standard print versions of this book may not be included in e-books or in print-on-demand. If this book refers to media such as a CD or DVD that is not included in the version you purchased, you may download this material at http://booksupport.wiley.com. For more information about Wiley products, visit www.wiley.com.

*Library of Congress Cataloging-in-Publication Data:*

Reynolds, Susan, 1949-
  Prescription for lasting success: leadership strategies to diagnose problems and transform your organization / Susan Reynolds.
    Includes index.
  ISBN 978-1-118-24142-4 (cloth); ISBN 978-1-118-28703-3 (ebk);
ISBN 978-1-118-28418-6 (ebk); ISBN 978-1-118-28310-3 (ebk)
  1. Leadership. 2. Strategic planning. 3. Organizational change. I. Title.
  HD57.7
  658.4–dc23
                                                                    2012015752

Printed in the United States of America.
10 9 8 7 6 5 4 3 2 1

*To my son, Chris Root, my greatest success!*

# CONTENTS

Acknowledgments                                                    xi

Introduction                                                        1
    Looking Beyond the Chief Complaint                        5
    What is *Success*?                                        8

**PART ONE**   **The Diagnosis from Outside-In: Assessing Your
Organization**                                                     11

CHAPTER 1   **Introducing the 4-Ps Model for Strategic
Transformation**                                                   13
    Defining the 4 Ps of Organizational Transformation        14
    Building a Dynamic Organization                           17
    Diagnosing Organizations from Outside-In                  17
    Looking Within an Organization                            19
    The 4 Ps for Organizational Transformation                20
    The Success of Apple                                      23
    Diagnosing and Treating                                   25

CHAPTER 2   **The 4 Ps and Effective Leadership: Assessing
Your Leadership Style**                                             27
    Defining the Four Aspects of Personal Health              28
    Leadership and Health                                     29

CHAPTER 3   **The 4 Ps and Organizational Transformation:
Assessing Your Organization**                                      35
    Look Beyond the Chief Complaint                           38
    Lasting Success                                           40

PART TWO   The Treatment from Inside Out: Transforming
Your Organization   43

CHAPTER 4   **Realigning Your Organization's Purpose and Core
Values**   **45**
Core Purpose: The Mission Statement   46
The Netflix Story: Changing Its Core Purpose   48
Core Values   50
*Core Values Gone Awry: The Wall Street Debacle*   51
*Core Values as Guideposts for Success: The Story of
Zappos*   52
Evolving Missions: Assessing Your Market   53
Personal Mission Statements   55
Changes in the Healthcare Industry   56

CHAPTER 5   **Restoring Passion in the Workplace**   **61**
The Effect of a Positive Attitude   62
The Effect of Negative Emotions   64
The Biochemistry of Emotion   65
Releasing Negative Emotions   66
*Dealing with Boredom*   66
*Resolving Anger*   68
*Dispelling Fear*   69
Recognizing Burnout   72
The Power of Positive Emotions   72
The Power of Caring   75
Passion in the Workplace   75

CHAPTER 6   **Creating and Communicating a Compelling
Organizational Vision**   **79**
The Importance of Vision in an Organization   81
Where Does Vision Come From?   83
Creating an Organizational Vision   85
Guided Imagery Exercise   86
Vision and Creative Problem Solving: Improving
Patient Satisfaction in the Emergency
Department   89
Communicating and Creating Buy-In to Your
Vision   90
Connecting with Your Audience   90

Listening 91
Building Rapport 94
Neuro-Linguistic Programming (NLP) 96
   *Are You Visual, Auditory, or Kinesthetic?* 98
   *NLP Mismatch* 100
Leading with Vision: The Story of Meriter Medical
   Group 101

CHAPTER 7   **Developing a Strategic Plan for Organizational
Transformation**   **105**
Internal and External Organizational Analysis 106
Goal Setting 107
The Working-Backwards Process 108
Developing Three to Five Specific Organizational
   Goals 109
Developing Two to Four Specific Objectives for
   Each Goal 110
Time: Create a Timeline for Each Step 110
Talent: Build Your Team 115
Treasure: Determine What Resources You Need 115
Do a Reality Check 116
Prioritizing Goals and Objectives 116
Remain Open to New Opportunities 117
Telling Others about Your Goals—A Word of
   Caution 118
Create a Feedback Loop to Assess Your Progress on
   a Quarterly Basis, and Adjust Your Plan
   Accordingly 119
Reward Your Team for Reaching Milestones 119
Personal Strategic Planning 120

CHAPTER 8   **Developing People, Transforming Your Culture**   **123**
The Value of the Right Human Capital 124
Motivating Others 126
Coaching to Improve Performance 127
Mentoring Generation Y 130
Building an Effective Team 132
Invest in People 135
The Power of Rewards 136
Physical Assets 137

CHAPTER 9    **Making Success Last: The 5th P, Perseverance**    **141**
The 5th P: Perseverance    142
Elements of Perseverance    145
*The Importance of Renewal*    147
Building versus Maintaining    149
The Time Frame Challenge    150
Perseverance in Business    150
Assessing Perseverance    152
*Personal Perseverance Scale*    153
*Organizational Perseverance Scale*    153
Improving Commitment    153
Improving Focus    154
Improving Endurance    154
Improving Renewal    155

CHAPTER 10    **The Final Prescription: A Strategic Transformation Summit**    **157**
Putting All 5 Ps Together    158
Pre-Summit Preparation    159
*Step 1: Choose the Right People to Participate in the Summit*    159
*Step 2: Do an Environmental Scan*    159
*Step 3: Do a SWOT Analysis. Identify Key Issues that Need to be Addressed*    160
*Step 4: Complete an Organizational Health Assessment*    160
The 5 Ps Summit    161
*Introduction: Give an Overview of the 5 Ps Process*    161
*The 1st P: Purpose and Core Values*    161
*The 2nd P: Passion*    162
*The 3rd P: Planning—Part 1: Vision*    163
*The 3rd P: Planning—Part 2: Setting Goals and Objectives*    164
*The 4th P: People and Physical Assets*    165
*The 5th P: Perseverance*    167
An Organization in Transformation: The California Medical Association    169
Transforming Your Organization    172

APPENDIX A    **Personal Health Assessment**                     **175**
        Personal Health Assessment                         176
          *Person: Physical Health*                        176
          *Planning: Mental Health*                        177
          *Passion: Emotional Health*                      178
          *Purpose: Spiritual Health*                      179
        Total Health Assessment Score                      180
        Interpretation of Scores                           180
          *Person: Physical Health*                        180
          *Planning: Mental Health*                        181
          *Passion: Emotional Health*                      181
          *Purpose: Spiritual Health*                      182
          *Total Health*                                   183

APPENDIX B    **Organizational Health Assessment**              **185**
        Organizational Health Assessment                   186
          *People and Physical Assets*                     186
          *Planning*                                       187
          *Passion*                                        188
          *Purpose*                                        189
        Total Organizational Health Assessment Score       190
        Interpretation of Scores                           190
          *People and Physical Assets*                     190
          *Planning*                                       191
          *Passion*                                        191
          *Purpose*                                        192
          *Total Organizational Health*                    193

Notes                                                            195

About the Author                                                 203

Index                                                            205

# ACKNOWLEDGMENTS

I was astounded when Adrianna Johnson, an acquisitions editor at John Wiley & Sons, made a cold call to me asking me to write a book after having found me on the Internet! For that Google search and her support during this entire process, I will always be deeply grateful to her. Her colleague at Wiley, Christine Moore, who has been my development editor during the writing of this book, has always been encouraging, letting me know that I am not just a public speaker, but also a writer. Thank you, Christine!

This book would not have been created without a considerable team effort. I am very grateful for the support I received from people with special talents and abilities beyond what I could do by myself. Thanks goes to Theresa Middlebrook and Linda Allderdice, my attorneys at Holland & Knight, who helped make sense of legal matters that were totally unfamiliar to me as a first-time author.

To William R. Heinke, my researcher, thank you for digging deep on the Internet. I am truly grateful for your thoroughness and persistence whether proofreading or tracking down references. I am especially grateful for your writing down all of the references in standard format, a task that seemed daunting to me.

Thank you to Tessa C. Carpenter, whose drawings are included in this book. You took my rough sketches and made them look professional. Your special talents in this area were a real gift to me.

To my exceptional proofreader, Elizabeth Fore Keatinge, I am grateful for your great eyesight, attention to detail, and knowledge of English grammar! Your edits and suggestions were quite helpful and meant a great deal to me.

I am very grateful to those people who allowed me to include their stories in this book including Mary Lou Licwinko, Executive Director of the San Francisco Medical Society; Dr. Robert Turngren, President of Meriter Medical Group; Dr. Martin Rossman, Co-Founder of The Academy for Guided Imagery; and Dustin Corcoran, CEO of the California Medical Association. Thanks also to Roger Purdy, Association Vice President at the California Medical Association, who encouraged me to research the CMA's story of ongoing transformation and include it in the book.

While writing the book, I received a great deal of support and encouragement from family and friends who deserve my heartfelt appreciation. I am grateful to my son, Chris Root, for always keeping my spirits up. To my sister, Kathie Rovetti, and my cousins Bill Highberger and Carolyn Kuhl, your input on key matters as well as your ongoing love and support has been invaluable. Thanks also to family friend Rex Heinke for his willingness to provide his advice and counsel, when asked.

Special thanks goes to Dr. Kim Wendelin, Chief Operating Officer of The Institute for Medical Leadership, who kept my company afloat while I was absorbed with writing the book. Special mention goes to Jeff Kramer, who along with Kim made sure our Chief of Staff Boot Camps continued with me out of the production loop. It is nice to know that I have a thriving business to come back to because of my exceptional staff as well as a dedicated faculty. I am grateful for all of your efforts.

Two faculty members deserve special mention for sharing their knowledge and expertise through programs The Institute for Medical Leadership has conducted. First, thanks very much to Dr. Richard Corlin, Past President of the American Medical Association, who has been an excellent sounding board for me, providing many astute observations about strategic planning as well as Generation Y. Also thanks to Dr. David Bresler, Co-Founder of The Academy for

Guided Imagery, who taught me visioning skills that have allowed me to become more creative and make this book a reality.

I am also grateful to the copyeditors and production staff at John Wiley who were truly professional as they turned my manuscript into a finished book.

One final thank you goes to Darlene Crist, who was my independent editor on a previous writing attempt eight years ago. Although that book was never published, Darlene gave me the confidence to say *"yes"* to John Wiley when the phone rang so unexpectedly last July.

Susan Reynolds, MD, PhD
Los Angeles, California
April 2012

# INTRODUCTION

*How do you measure success? To laugh often, and much; to win the respect of intelligent people and the affection of children; to earn the appreciation of honest critics and endure the betrayal of false friends; to appreciate beauty; to find the best in others; to leave the world a bit better, whether by a healthy child, a redeemed social condition, or a job well done; to know even one other life has breathed because you lived—this is to have succeeded.*

—Ralph Waldo Emerson

Two events that took place in the early 1990s made me abruptly change the direction of my career, which shifted away from that of emergency physician and owner of an emergency medical center, toward that of a headhunter, executive coach, and organizational development consultant. The first event occurred in 1993 when I was appointed to the White House Health Professionals Review Group, which consisted of 44 healthcare providers invited by Hillary Rodham Clinton to critique her health plan as it was being formulated.

I noticed at the time of my White House appointment that 80 days had already passed since the inception of Clinton's plan and the formation of her task force—and approximately 500 healthcare think tank type "experts" had already drafted a sweeping plan to reform the U.S. healthcare system. None of these people appeared to be in a clinical practice where they were seeing patients for a

1

living. I also noticed that only 8 of the 44 individuals in our Review Group were physicians in active clinical practice, doctors who were earning the majority of their income from seeing patients.

Our group was brought in at the level of what was called Tollgate 5—the fifth checkpoint in the process of plan development set up by chief healthcare policy advisor Ira Magaziner. We were allowed to comment, critique, or challenge anything that had already passed through four other Tollgates. We could also submit new ideas, as long as we kept each idea on only one page. However, it was quite evident that the train was already leaving the station, so to speak, and we barely had time to jump on and review—or merely rubber stamp—what the think tank experts had already created.

Of course, it was an honor to have been selected to participate on a White House Review Group. However, the experience made me realize that practicing physicians were not in the lead during such proceedings; in fact, they seemed more like an afterthought as massive changes to the healthcare system were being proposed. The lack of leadership from practicing physicians seemed like a terrible oversight to me. I wanted to do something to assure that practicing physicians were at least at the table as the healthcare system was reformed, but it was not obvious how to proceed at that point in time.

The second life-altering event—a series of events, actually—occurred between 1993 and 1994. I had built and was the sole owner of the Malibu Emergency Room and Family Medical Center, and ran it in a community that didn't have a hospital from 1982 to 1994. In the absence of adequate Los Angeles County funding, I had worked with community leaders and local celebrities to set up a tax-exempt charity that produced rock concerts and dinner galas to support emergency medical care. Tragically, four natural disasters hit our town between February 7, 1993, and February 7, 1994—destroying the area and ruining my business. There was first severe flooding, then fire, followed by an earthquake, and, finally, mudslides—the effects of which forced my business to close in the spring of 1994. It was a heartbreaking time in my life, made even worse by the fact that this professional turmoil occurred shortly after my divorce from my husband—the father of my son and an entertainment attorney to whom I had been married for 7 years.

I decided not to file for bankruptcy; however, I needed money to pay off my debts, pay my mortgage, and keep my son in private school. So I took a job as an executive search consultant (i.e., a headhunter) at Heidrick & Struggles, the second-largest executive search firm in the world. At the time, I thought I had landed on Mars. After eighteen-and-a-half years as an emergency physician, I had jettisoned myself out of the world of emergency medicine only to land in the bizarre and completely unfamiliar world of big business and executive search.

Although much of my first day at Heidrick is now a blur, I remember quite vividly having my boss inform me that we headhunters were in "the leadership business." I smiled and nodded agreement, but really wasn't at all sure what he meant by that phrase. Having always been a good student, I decided to run down to Borders bookstore that afternoon, thinking I would find a book or two on the subject of leadership. Much to my amazement, I found an entire section filled with dozens of books on the topic.

My first thought was that we certainly didn't cover this topic in medical school. My second thought was, "Where do I begin?" There were a couple of titles that were familiar to me—Stephen R. Covey's perennial bestseller *The 7 Habits of Highly Effective People*, first published in 1989, as well as *Principled Centered Leadership*, also by Covey, and published the following year. But there were *so many more*. John Gardner's *On Leadership*, and *On Becoming a Leader* by Warren Bennis seemed like good books to begin with as I started my leadership studies.

I began to read everything I could find about leadership theory, styles, characteristics, and skills—basically anything that had the word leadership in it. I recalled vividly how the practicing physicians were *not* in the lead during my days at the White House. With a heightened awareness that we physicians were not taught much about this area during medical school, I decided to delve into the leadership literature and make myself a quasi-expert on this topic. I knew I could become at least more knowledgeable than many of my physician colleagues and could then teach some of them what I had learned.

I used my newfound expertise on leadership to eventually create a leadership training institute for the American Medical Association. I based the curriculum on a market analysis I had done of physicians' career needs. However, the AMA did not share my vision of what needed to be taught; they spun off the institute in its second year, giving me cash and the copyright. Yet what had initially seemed like a loss turned out to be a major blessing in my life; I launched and now own The Institute for Medical Leadership. To date, The Institute has provided leadership development programs, executive coaching services, executive searches, and strategic planning retreats in 38 states for hundreds of organizations—primarily hospitals, health systems, and medical societies and also insurance companies and law firms.

My life has certainly had its ups and downs, and at times has seemed like an E-ticket ride at Disneyland. There have been moments of great successes—including the birth of my son, academic honors, a career as an emergency physician, celebrity rock concerts, and a White House appointment. But there have also been instances of great loss, like my divorce and the loss of the Malibu Emergency Room. Ultimately, however, these hardships dramatically transformed my life and career—and I found an unexpected increase in both my personal happiness and professional success.

I learned quite a few lessons from my business loss in Malibu. As I moved away from the clinical world of emergency medicine and into the world of business and organizational development, I found that certain concepts I had used to alter my life and career very successfully could also be applied to transform the companies that were now my clients. I also discovered that I could diagnose what ails a company in a manner that is analogous to diagnosing a sick patient.

## Looking Beyond the Chief Complaint

My clinical experience had taught me that it was very important for a physician to look beyond the chief complaint when diagnosing any ailment. When patients see a physician, they always state a reason for why they have come. Perhaps it is an ankle injury, headache, or seizure. Their presenting problem is called the chief complaint. After treating tens of thousands of patients over an 18-year period, I learned that most patients did not come to see me solely because of their chief complaints; they often had more significant issues that needed to be addressed. If I did not tend to these other less obvious factors—that were frequently the cause of the chief complaint—the patients would be back to see me before long. I might give them a pill or prescribe some other therapy for their ailments, but if we didn't get to the heart of the matter and deal with the chief complaint's underlying cause, they would eventually return with recurring symptoms or a new complaint.

In the first year after natural disasters had destroyed the Malibu Emergency Room, and before I became a headhunter, I was the Director of Ambulatory Care for a medical group in Santa Monica, California, where I had several physicians, nurses, and physician assistants working with me. In an attempt to get beyond the chief complaint, I suggested that we all ask three extra questions of every patient that came to see us. The questions were simple: "How are things going?" (a very general question by design), followed by "How is your job going?," and ending with "How is your relationship with your significant other and/or your family?"

Patients' answers were quite amazing, and we became convinced that our patients did not come to see us simply for toothaches, headaches, or sprained ankles. There were countless additional reasons that prompted them to take time off from work or away from other responsibilities to make the trip to the doctor's office and tell someone what was bothering them.

My favorite example of looking beyond the chief complaint was the case of a woman who had come to the ambulatory care center with sinusitis seven times in eight months. She kept coming back with sinus congestion and a great deal of pain in her head. On each visit, she was examined by a physician or physician assistant who sometimes would order sinus X-rays; but she ultimately received an antibiotic to treat the infection, and a decongestant to reduce congestion and relieve the pain. Though she would always recover, she would be back after a few weeks with a new episode.

On her seventh visit for sinusitis, one of my physician assistants asked me to see her; she had found by way of the three extra questions that the patient hated her job. She was having a horrible conflict with her boss, but had never discussed it with her. The funny thing was that this conflict had been going on for about eight months—the same duration as the recurrent sinusitis episodes.

When I saw her, I went through some things she could do to improve her working relationship with her boss—a little career counseling along with some pills to clear her latest infection. Interestingly, I never saw her again. At the time, I thought her lack of recurrent visits could have been because the school district where she worked had changed health coverage, or I thought perhaps she had found the courage to quit her job.

Six months later, a friend of mine called and said, "I don't know what you said to my daughter, but you changed her life." At first, I drew a blank and did not know who his daughter was, but as he relayed the story, I learned that his daughter was the woman with sinusitis (she had a different last name). He told me that she had taken my suggestion and talked to her boss about her concerns. Her boss had been totally unaware of any problem between them, and they were able to resolve their differences once the issue was out in the open. My friend's daughter was promoted, received a raise—and never had sinusitis again.

This case made me realize that there was much more to diagnosing and treating a patient than just addressing the presenting problem, the chief complaint. Each time, the patient had been diagnosed and treated appropriately, given her physical complaint. We had simply been doing what we had been trained to do; that is, focus primarily on the physical ailments and find a way to fix them. Until we asked those three extra questions, we knew little about other aspects of a patient's health, including her mental, emotional, and spiritual states. Only by probing deeper were we able to get to the real reason she had developed physical symptoms. With this information, we then could help her heal completely—and in so doing, improve her life and career.

Another example of how addressing solely the chief complaint may fail to heal completely is the case of a patient who complained of an inability to sleep. I completed a thorough review of systems as part of his medical history, which revealed no obvious cause for his sleep disturbance. This patient came in about six months after a very damaging Northridge, California, earthquake, which had registered 6.7 on the Richter scale, and something told me that I should ask him how he had fared during the natural disaster. It turned out that he had been awakened from sleep by the noise and the shaking of the quake. He had jumped out of bed and barely avoided being killed by a falling mirror that had come crashing down off his bedroom wall.

This patient's sleep disturbance had begun right after this traumatic incident; however, he had forgotten about it until I asked him about the earthquake. No sleep medication would have been effective in treating his symptoms; he needed to undergo emotional healing to return to a normal sleeping pattern. A clinical psychologist treated the patient briefly to resolve his earthquake-related emotional trauma, which in turn resolved his sleep disturbance.

Many similar experiences in treating patients led me to become more holistic in my approach to health and healing. I also realized that although I was diagnosing my patients from outside-in—beginning with the physical, then the mental, then the emotional, and finally the spiritual aspects of health—the healing process frequently took place in reverse: from inside-out.

As I changed my career from clinical medicine to the world of business, replacing my black bag and stethoscope with a black briefcase and laptop, I came to realize that organizations are made up of people, and therefore have four analogous aspects of health that can be diagnosed and treated to bring about organizational transformation. Chapter 1 of this book describes the process I have developed, which I call the 4 Ps of Strategic Transformation: Purpose, Passion, Planning, and People (the 4-Ps model).

I've adopted common business terms in my model to represent the four aspects of organizational health and well-being. *Purpose* is used to represent the *spirit* of an organization; *Passion* represents its *emotions*; *Planning* represents the *mental* aspect; and *People* represent the *physical* aspect of organizational health and prosperity.

Chapter 2 looks at how the health of an organization's leader can affect the health of the entire organization. Readers are invited to take a personal health assessment using the 4-Ps model to determine whether any aspect of their own health and well-being is out of balance, potentially impeding their effectiveness as an organizational leader. Chapter 3 encourages readers to use the 4-Ps model to diagnose their own organization and determine if any aspect is out of balance and in need of treatment.

Having learned the 4-Ps model and assessed yourself and your organization in Part One of this book, Part Two will present transformation strategies to maximize your long-lasting personal and organizational success, with the recommended approach to transformation taking place from inside out.

## What is *Success*?

Any book on *success* should include at some point a definition of what it means to be successful. *Merriam-Webster's Collegiate Dictionary* (www.merriam-webster.com) calls success "a favorable or desired outcome" or "the attainment of wealth, favor, or eminence." For more than a decade, corporate America has been rocked with scandal after scandal, with greed and avarice destroying the public's trust in long-standing financial institutions, some of which no longer exist. Therefore, I do not believe that amassing money for money's sake can truly be called success.

My working definition of *success* for this book is to attain set goals and objectives that allow an organization to grow, while providing much needed products and services to its marketplace. (Personally, I prefer Emerson's definition at the beginning of this introduction.) In my experience, success implies happiness, a feeling of accomplishment, a sense of pride in obtaining a desired outcome, and an opportunity to be of service to at least one other person.

This book is about success, but not just any success—*lasting* success. A lot of authors provide success strategies for individuals and organizations, and the world is full of one-hit wonders. Being able to sustain success is a far more challenging matter, and requires more than a quick fix to achieve. For lasting success, there is a fifth P—Perseverance. Chapter 9 will discuss ways to incorporate perseverance into your corporate culture, making it a part of your ongoing renewal process. Without it, organizational transformation may occur, but will not be sustained over the long run.

The focus of this book is corporate transformation, but it is based on what I have learned by going through my own personal transformation at the hands of Mother Nature. The inside-out healing process was a key factor in my own success, and as I worked with organizations, I found that I could use a similar process to diagnose and transform them. The chapters that follow will outline how to diagnose what ails your organization. You will then be given a formula—a *prescription*, really—for bringing about change in the areas that are weak. In Chapter 10 you will be given a final prescription, which outlines what I call a *strategic transformation summit* that uses all five Ps to maximize your lasting personal and organizational success.

# PART ONE

# The Diagnosis from Outside-In: Assessing Your Organization

CHAPTER

1

# Introducing the 4-Ps Model for Strategic Transformation

*Some people dream of success . . . while others wake up and work hard at it.*

—Anonymous

When I became an organizational development consultant, I had years of experience as an emergency physician under my belt. I used this knowledge to develop a strategy for diagnosing and treating "poor health" in underperforming organizations—a strategy that was modeled after what I had used to diagnose and treat sick individuals. I also knew that my emergency room's "illness"—and subsequent closure, due partially to the stress of four natural disasters hitting in a single year—had knocked my own health off balance. As I mentioned in the introduction, I developed a model to diagnose and treat problems in unhealthy organizations, which I call the 4 Ps of Strategic Transformation: Purpose, Passion, Planning, and People (the 4-Ps model).

Since physicians are trained to begin a patient assessment by evaluating physical symptoms, it was easiest for me to diagnose "illness" in an organization from outside-in. However, I knew I had to dig deeper to find the root cause of the presenting problems. I also came to realize—as both a physician and as an organizational consultant—that any treatment or return to organizational health and prosperity needs to incorporate all 4 Ps, and take place from inside out.

As a headhunter, I began each executive search by conducting an organizational assessment. I felt that this helped me to better ascertain the duties and responsibilities of a successful candidate, and also to understand what the organizational culture was like. I found the 4 Ps, analogous to the four aspects of personal health, in every organization. Sometimes they were functioning well, but at other times at least one of them was causing problems—either localized in a specific work area, or having spread like a virus to various parts of the organization.

## Defining the 4 Ps of Organizational Transformation

So how do we break down the four aspects of an organization that are analogous to the four components of personal health and well-being? The *physical* element obviously includes a company's bricks and mortar, equipment, finances, and reserves. But the most important physical aspect is the *People*, or an organization's human capital: employees, management personnel, administrative leaders, and members of the board of directors. An organization can have a great concept, an impressive implementation strategy, and money in the bank, but if it has the wrong people on board—or the right people in the wrong positions—it will not flourish and maximize its success.

The *mental* part of an organization is its *Planning*, which includes its visioning process, strategic planning with the setting of goals and objectives, and the intellectual capital that comes from the thought processes or creative energies of those who work there. Is creativity allowed to thrive? Do the organization's leaders encourage out-of-the-box thinking? Or is there too much red tape, too many policies and procedures, for new ideas and processes to surface and take hold?

The *emotional* aspect of an organization involves interpersonal relationships, and is reflected in whether or not employees feel *Passion* for their work. The way that leaders communicate throughout the organization greatly influences its culture—and the positive or negative energy associated with it. For example, problems like poor communication or power struggles can cause a great deal of anger to build up within an organization. Simple, seemingly harmless snafus—such as leaving a voice mail for someone who only checks his or her e-mail—can build tension and lead to a perceived lack of communication between two people who need to work well together. Frequently, such scenarios also cause fiefdoms to develop. These are situations in which people who feel disempowered and misinformed band together. In some cases, fiefdoms compete so intensely with one another that all communication breaks down and organizational esprit de corps is destroyed.

The *spirit* of an organization resides in its core *Purpose*, or mission—that is, why it does what it does. What business is it in? Purpose also implies service to others. Does the organization truly serve its customer's needs? For example, I know that I am in the teaching business, and specifically the physician leadership-development business. I know that national healthcare reform has prompted a huge need for effective physician leadership that focuses on improving the quality of healthcare and patient satisfaction, while reducing cost. So my business of educating doctors to be effective leaders is definitely in sync with the marketplace—and steadily growing.

Spirit also includes a firm's values and organizational integrity as well as its service to others. When the company can clearly state these elements—and practice them from top to bottom—its spirit will be in good working order. But unfortunately, many organizations lose sight of their mission somewhere along the way. Many fail to keep up with a changing marketplace and don't realize that their long-standing mission may no longer serve their customers' needs. Or, as in the case of the demise of major Wall Street institutions such as Lehman Brothers and Bear Stearns, a complete lack of organizational integrity brought about institutional demise.

Organizational integrity is undermined when a leader's actions do not match his or her words. For example, a hospital CEO might present certain quality and performance figures to the hospital board, but share different or watered-down information with the medical staff. This lack of transparency can result in a breakdown of integrity. It's essential in order for an organization to prosper to get back in touch with purpose and reestablish organizational integrity.

Each of the 4 Ps must be functioning well in order for an organization to maximize success. The most successful organizations establish a mission that is in sync with its customer base (Purpose); can overcome emotional barriers to creativity and growth (Passion); have a clear vision and strategic plan for the future (Planning); and have healthy human capital and plentiful financial reserves in work environments that foster productivity (People).

A fifth P, Perseverance—to which we alluded in the introduction—is crucial for maintaining long-lasting success. Organizations need to develop an ongoing process of renewal that enables them to achieve optimal success on a long-term basis. Without the element of perseverance, success may be only a flash in the pan, fading quickly due to a lack of sustained focus and commitment to achieving the corporate vision, goals, and objectives. I have come to realize in working with my clients that organizations must consider Perseverance at the end of any assessment of organizational health that uses the 4-Ps model.

## Building a Dynamic Organization

I have conducted a variety of workshops and strategic planning retreats over the past decade with the title, "Building a Dynamic Organization." These programs have proved to be quite popular; problems of organizational stagnation and lack of productivity are apparently quite common, no matter what industry or company size. I use the 4-Ps model at these programs to help organizations assess and determine exactly what is not working. I then guide them to make strategic changes by aligning the 4 Ps for maximal success.

I found after leading several of these sessions that not only can the 4 Ps be used to guide the organization as a whole, but company members can also apply them to divisions, to work teams, and even individual committees. It's vital that all of these subdivisions understand how the 4 Ps apply to their:

1. **Purpose:** Why do they exist? What is their mission within the company?
2. **Passion:** Are team members or committee members really *passionate* about what they do?
3. **Planning:** Do they have a planning process with goals and objectives for their group that meshes with the organization's overall strategic plan?
4. **People:** Are the right people on the team—and in the right positions?

They must also consider their capacity to **Persevere:** Does their culture engender an ongoing renewal process to maintain lasting success?

## Diagnosing Organizations from Outside-In

My unique perspective as a physician also led me to see that companies can diagnose organizational health and well-being in a similar way to individual health: from outside-in, beginning with the presenting problem. Science and technology can help in this assessment as they can with personal health—but only up to a point. The overall assessment will be limited unless you go beyond what technology can offer and use other techniques to determine what's ailing your organization.

As in medicine, it is important to look beyond what we call your organization's chief complaint such as a decline in sales or membership, a loss in revenue for other reasons, or high staff turnover. While you may not refer to this issue as the chief complaint, you will recognize it as the presenting problem—one to which you must pay attention to restore health and profitability to your organization. It could be that sales are dropping off, or you are using reserves to cover operating losses, or staff morale is poor, or equipment outdated, or your recent advocacy or marketing campaign was not effective. Whatever the problem is, there may well be other factors that need to be considered before you can lead your organization to peak performance.

Many diagnostic tools are available to assess organizations including (but not limited to) financial audits, management assessments, 360-degree employee evaluations, personality testing such as the Myers-Briggs, equipment inventories, and Lean/Six Sigma performance improvement processes. However, while they are no doubt valuable to some degree, each of these methods is limited in scope and tends to focus on an organization's physical aspects (i.e., finances, equipment, and human capital).

A true assessment of an organization's well-being must look deeper and also include a review of its mission, purpose, core values, culture, methods of communication, vision, and strategic plan—in other words, all 4 Ps. It must also consider the organization's capacity to persevere in the long run. Each element requires that you listen carefully and gather input from many stakeholders, which can become time-consuming. Although this kind of an in-depth assessment might seem like a luxury in a competitive marketplace, it is vital for organizational success.

## Looking Within an Organization

I did a lot of organizational development consulting for the American Medical Association (AMA) during my headhunting days. This once highly-revered—and, in fact, feared because of its political clout—organization was a "must-join" for almost all physicians in the United States. In fact, in the 1950s approximately 75 percent of physicians in the United States belonged to the AMA.[1] However, over time, the AMA has stagnated, losing members year after year, and replacing dwindling dues with nondues revenue, even selling real estate holdings in order to stay afloat. In spite of launching new membership campaigns and developing new products that the association's business managers had predicted physicians would buy, membership has continued to drop, even to this day. An AMA long-range planning document presented at the AMA's 2011 Annual Meeting reveals that by December 2010 only about 15 percent of practicing U.S. physicians were AMA members.[2]

The AMA's declining membership is multifactorial, and while many organizations have lost members in recent years due to generational change and technology, it hasn't been to the degree that the AMA has experienced. We can use the 4-Ps model to determine where the AMA may have lost its way—at least as far as its membership is concerned—in an attempt to better understand and diagnose the group's difficulties. The chief complaint, or presenting problem, seems to be membership decline, which is a people problem. In the simplest of terms, doctors are not joining the AMA, and former members are not renewing their memberships. They clearly do not see any value in remaining members. It must be remembered, of course, that back in its heyday the AMA was the only medical/political organization, but now there are more than 100 medical societies representing various physician interests.

The AMA lists national strategic planning issues on its website that include items like "cost of healthcare," "quality of care," "access and workforce issues," "next generation physician payment," and "prevention and wellness." Something's obviously missing here, as there does not seem to be any focus on increasing membership.

I have worked for over 25 associations, and have found that in most cases people join organizations because of *people*, not because of issues. The AMA's de facto strategic plan focuses on increasing nondues revenue, a strategy that has proven to be quite successful for 11 years in a row while membership has declined.

The passion physicians feel for the AMA actually has both positive and negative repercussions; the AMA frequently takes on controversial political issues that can be divisive, even within the physician community. Having a divided, though, passionate membership like this makes it difficult to rally positive forces that would enable the organization to grow and prosper. The 12,000 physicians who terminated their AMA membership in 2010 were passionate about opposing the Affordable Care Act (i.e., "Obamacare"), which the AMA supported. So negative passion can be very destructive.

We must also consider purpose. What business is the AMA in? Is it truly serving current and potential members' needs? Is it staying true to its core purpose over time? Does it need to alter that core purpose due to a changing environment?

And finally, after assessing the 4 Ps of organizational health, we must evaluate the AMA's ability to persevere in spite of challenging roadblocks that limit the organization's success.

## The 4 Ps for Organizational Transformation

We can apply the 4 Ps to the AMA example to show how such an organization can be transformed to new levels of success and prosperity. Though all 4 Ps might need attention in this case, it is best to begin the transformation from inside out and first evaluate the organization's Purpose. The following mission statement appears on the AMA's website and indicates its core purpose:

> *"to promote the art and science of medicine and the betterment of public health."*

This mission—at least, in part—dates back to 1847, when the AMA was founded. However, it has (not surprisingly) lost some of its impact over time and been replaced by the AMA's de facto mission of advocacy work in Washington, lobbying legislators for better reimbursement for physicians and myriad other issues.

It occurred to me that since doctors are in the profession of health and healing, physicians who are AMA members, former members, and nonmembers might relate better to a mission statement that includes elements that mention health, healing, and success. After reviewing the recent AMA Annual Report, I determined that its purpose has become more focused on finding new sources of nondues revenue rather than helping doctors succeed in the ever-changing healthcare arena. If the AMA's true mission were more in sync with the needs of its potential members—as is the case with specialty medical societies that provide continuing education—it would increase membership and be able to build a more successful organization that would continue to grow its membership.

If there is no unifying purpose, then perhaps the AMA needs to evaluate what business it needs to be in. Should it remain a membership organization or become an organization of organizations (i.e., an umbrella for all of the state and specialty medical societies)? Perhaps it should develop a medical/political coordinating council of medical societies in order to become more meaningful to all physicians.

When an organization's purpose is not in sync with its prospective members' needs, no membership drive will be effective. You probably want to ask yourself if you are looking for more members or customers: Is our mission up-to-date? Is it relevant, considering current market conditions? Would it *really* attract new members or customers? If sales are down in spite of a great sales force and a great sales strategy, there may be a problem with your organization's purpose. So figure out if there's a real need for what you are trying to sell—and whether your purpose and mission are aligned with your market. There may be misalignment if the marketplace is changing.

Resolving its passion issues will always be one of the AMA's greatest challenges, since by their very natures, doctors are healers

rather than fighters. Had their innate personalities been more com-
bative, they may have chosen to go to law school instead of medical
school. Yet the AMA seems to attract the most argumentative type
of physicians—those who like the challenge of policy debates. At
one point, the AMA even hired a former USAF fighter pilot as its
CEO, a physician warrior who ended up attacking the AMA with
a major lawsuit as he left the organization after only three years.

Planning at the AMA should ideally incorporate an overarching
vision that includes all physicians, no matter what their specialty,
mode of practice, or policy perspective. The AMA's vision, as touted
on its website, includes the aim "To be an essential part of the professional life of every physician." This is a great vision, indeed. Yet
year after year, the AMA hasn't seemed to be able to develop a
strategy to make this vision a reality. They can't seem to retain current members, or get new ones to join, so they have not become an
essential element in physicians' professional lives.

The People aspect of the AMA has had its fair share of issues as
well. Besides the type of physicians it attracts, the AMA appeared
to be—in my experience, at least—one of the most internally
siloed organizations with which I have ever worked. Any inter-silo
communication between competent professionals was limited at
best—and stymied by processes at worst. For example, I was tasked
with designing a brochure for a joint program I was conducting
for the AMA and the California Medical Association (CMA). I
therefore needed both association logos for the brochure cover.
While the CMA staff emailed me their logo within 30 minutes of
my request, the AMA took three weeks to send theirs, telling me at
one point that their legal department had to give its OK for the use
of the color and the font in its logo. This high degree of red tape
only blocks such an organization's flow of productive innovation
and out-of-the-box thinking. Even when you have talented people
who are trying to do an excellent job, it will be difficult for the
organization to maximize its success.

The AMA example demonstrates how important it is to look
beyond the chief complaint or the presenting problem and see what's

truly lurking under the surface. In order to transform an organization such as the AMA, you must assess all 4 Ps and treat the ones that need it. It's best to conduct this kind of diagnosis from outside-in, beginning with the obvious problem such as declining membership. However, transformation needs to come from inside out in order to ensure that the right people sufficiently address any underlying problems to prevent relapses. This inside-out approach begins in the AMA example by reevaluating the mission to clarify what business they are in and whom they are serving, then developing positive passion throughout the organization that will lead to the development of a compelling vision and planning process. The AMA must also put the right people in the right positions to execute the plan, breaking down silos that have been barriers to change. And finally, they must critically evaluate the organization's ability to persevere, even in the most challenging times.

## The Success of Apple

Apple provides a timely example of how all 4 Ps in an organization can work cohesively to create a hugely successful company. The company is perhaps best known for its visionary CEO, Steve Jobs—whose passing on October 5, 2011 was mourned by millions around the world. Deemed "The Inventor of the Future" by *Time* Magazine,[3] Jobs led Apple to huge financial success, leading it to become the world's most valuable company in August 2011 (valued at \$337 billion).[4] Most importantly, Apple is also known for providing truly visionary products to its customers, selling millions of Macs, iPods, iPhones, and iPads around the globe.

We can assess the 4 Ps at Apple by first reviewing its Purpose. The following mission statement is posted on Apple's Investor Relations FAQ page:

> *Apple designs Macs, the best personal computers in the world, along with OS X, iLife, iWork, and professional software. Apple leads the digital music revolution with its iPods and iTunes online store.*

*Apple reinvented the mobile phone with its revolutionary iPhone and App Store, and has recently introduced its magical iPad which is defining the future of mobile media and computing devices.*

This statement could be summarized to say that Apple's purpose is to design innovative products that revolutionize personal communications and transform industries through cutting-edge technology. It's clear to anyone that Apple has stayed true to its stated purpose as its success has exponentially grown.

The Passion that Apple employees and customers feel for its revolutionary products is palpable. Just walk into any Apple Store the next time you pass by, and you'll immediately sense the positive energy from staff members and visitors alike.

Jobs' visionary leadership has clearly prompted Apple to become a company filled with out-of-the box ideas and creative solutions. But in addition to vision, careful Planning had to be in place in order to execute that vision successfully on a global scale time and time again.

Apple employs incredibly bright and talented individuals who have also been inspired by Jobs' leadership to give their best efforts to the company. In fact, Jobs' product launches have had an almost cult-like atmosphere about them. One of the most remarkable forces behind Apple's success is its ability to design products that people want and are easy to use. The company's focus on People has therefore been critical to its success.

The 5th P, Perseverance, is the final element that helps guarantee lasting success. Apple has had its ups and downs, but has triumphed over time because of the presence of all 4 Ps *and* Perseverance.

The question of what will happen to Apple after Jobs' passing remains on many people's minds. Will the brand continue to be visionary, anticipating changes in the market before they occur? Will the creative spirit still thrive within the company? Will the people within the company, as well as its customers, remain inspired and passionate about their work and future Apple products?

# Diagnosing and Treating

We will take a closer look at how Jobs' failing health impacted his company in Chapter 2, where we discuss health as a leadership trait. That chapter will also give you the opportunity to use the 4 Ps—Purpose, Passion, Planning, and People—to assess your own health and ability as a leader. While this isn't an in-depth health assessment, it should give you some clues about areas that might be out of balance.

Chapter 3 will invite you to complete an organizational assessment, again using the 4 Ps model. This diagnostic tool is meant to provide you with an overview of certain aspects of your organization's well-being that you may need to address. It is *not* meant to provide an in-depth analysis of all of your organization's woes. But it should, at the very least, indicate which areas are most problematic and need immediate attention.

Part Two of this book presents strategies for using each of the 4 Ps to transform your organization in order to have it thrive, even in difficult economic times. In Chapter 9, I'll discuss the 5th P, Perseverance, and the role of renewal in your organization. It's vital to remember that transformation starts from inside out, by objectively evaluating your organization's mission statement and core values. Are they still relevant for the current market? Do you need to update them—or perhaps throw them out altogether?

Once your organization's purpose and core values are clear, you have to treat its culture. You want to eliminate fiefdoms and remove any cultural or communication barriers that are causing emotional blocks before you can establish a compelling vision and strategic plan for your company. Again, if purpose has drifted and passion is lacking, it would be best to delay development of a new vision and strategic plan because the end result will be suboptimal. Remove the blocks first; then move on to create a great envisioned future.

Once you have aligned Purpose, Passion, and Planning within your organization, you will probably find that at least some People problems are far less problematic—and may have even disappeared. Any remaining problems will be much easier to address. You must then be sure that Perseverance is part of your corporate culture to assure long-lasting success.

Of course, you cannot transform your organization by yourself; you absolutely must include other key stakeholders in the process. At the end of Part Two, I outline a strategic transformation summit, which you can use as a template for a process to improve your leadership effectiveness and bring about organizational transformation, regardless of your organization's size. It will help you include key people in the 4-Ps diagnosis and treatment processes and the 5th-P process of ongoing renewal, so that your people maximize their contributions to your organization's overall success.

# The 4 Ps and Effective Leadership: Assessing Your Leadership Style

*A wise man should consider that health is the greatest of human blessings . . . .*

—Hippocrates

When I began to work with organizations' leaders and reviewed a lot of the leadership literature, I wondered if, somehow, a leader's personal health would be reflected in the organization's health. That is, if one area of a leader's health were out of balance, would that same area be out of balance in the organization he or she led? And would a leader's own healing process lead to transformation within his or her organization—thereby increasing its performance and productivity?

A recent example of a leader with significant health issues is the late Steve Jobs, former CEO of Apple. Diagnosed with an operable type of pancreatic cancer in October 2003, Jobs postponed his surgery for nine months, while stockholders and board members got very nervous. He did not make his illness public until August 1, 2004, right after he had surgery to remove the tumor. By keeping his condition under wraps until it was presumed to be successfully treated, Jobs prompted investors to focus on Apple's new innovative products rather than his illness, thus having a negligible effect on Apple's stock value.

In fact, if anything, the announcement that Jobs' cancer surgery had been successful helped spark new creative product development, as well as a worldwide sales effort—and profits soared. Apple had become the world's most valuable company (valued at $337 billion) in August 2011—seven years after Jobs' initial surgery[1]—having sold millions of products around the globe. While the effect that Jobs' 2011 death will have on Apple remains to be seen, analysts predict that there are enough of his innovative ideas in the pipeline that the company will continue to prosper—at least in the short run.

## Defining the Four Aspects of Personal Health

Before assessing how leaders' health can impact the enterprises they oversee, we must first understand the four aspects of personal health: the physical, mental, emotional, and spiritual elements. Each of these is analogous to one of the 4 Ps in the 4-Ps organizational model presented in Chapter 1. It is necessary to balance these four areas in order to maximize your leadership effectiveness; only then will you live a healthy and fulfilling life, and be able to guide your organization to optimal success.

The physical realm obviously pertains to the health of the physical body, which is affected by any number of ailments. We can call this aspect the Person, analogous to People in the 4 Ps. This also includes the physical environment in which a person lives, and should prompt people to consider questions like: Is your home or office cluttered or dirty? Is there a sense of balance or harmony in the space around you? Finances can also affect physical health. Is your checkbook balanced? Do you have a regular savings plan? Are you set for retirement? All of these elements are important to consider when assessing one's personal health status on a physical level.

The mental aspect of health pertains to your thoughts, mindset, and beliefs; any habits or behaviors you tend to repeat, or actions that may limit your ability to reach goals and objectives. It is analogous to Planning in the 4-Ps model. Do you have a vision for your life? Are you following that plan, and updating it at regular intervals?

The emotional realm is the realm of feelings: How do you react to others? What is the nature of your interpersonal relationships? Do you feel passion for your work? Are you angry about events or people in the past? Are you fearful of a potential future event? Are you still recovering from a significant loss? This aspect is equivalent to Passion in the 4-Ps model.

The spiritual realm includes your inner world, sense of purpose or personal mission, values, principles, and personal integrity. If your actions do not match what you believe is the right thing to do—or if you don't feel aligned with your life purpose—you can experience major stress, causing your effectiveness as a leader to suffer. In the 4 Ps, the spiritual realm is called Purpose.

## Leadership and Health

Several experts cite the importance of physical health in their writings about effective leadership. Author John Gardner listed "physical vitality and stamina" as one of his 14 leadership characteristics in his classic book *On Leadership*.[2] In the Drucker Foundation's essay collection on this topic entitled *The Leader of the Future*,

Richard J. Leider, founder of a training firm called The Inventure Group in Minneapolis, gives a series of 20 tips on self-leadership for would-be leaders. Interestingly, his first tip mentions physical, mental, and emotional symptoms.

> *"Recognize your stress level. Watch for signs of stress—forgetfulness; chronic fatigue; sleeplessness; changes in appetite; increased colds, headaches, or lower back pain; withdrawal from relationships; or increased mood swings. If you aren't sure you have a problem, ask your family and friends whether they have noticed changes in you."*[3]

Leider understands that any of these symptoms can be warning signs for leaders that should prompt them to pay attention to any potential stress in their working environment.

Chronic stress can lead to poor health in both individuals and organizations. The Yerkes-Dodson Law, formulated by two physiologists in 1908 and illustrated in Figure 2.1, states that as stress increases, so does productivity, but only up to a certain point. After that point, any further increase in stress leads to a *decrease* in a person's performance:

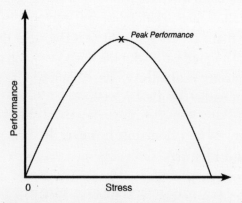

**Figure 2.1   Yerkes-Dodson Law**

*Source:* R. M. Yerkes and J. D. Dodson.[4]

The same holds true for organizations. Some degree of pressure to meet certain deadlines can help individuals and groups perform better; however, excessive stress in the workplace will diminish motivation and cause energy levels to fall and productivity to decrease. I have seen this scenario unfold many times—and unless someone takes action to reduce stress levels, the organization suffers.

For example, let's say that a hospital anticipates an unannounced visit from The Joint Commission (TJC) to evaluate their accreditation status. In this scenario, the team responsible for meeting TJC standards is under a great deal of pressure, especially since the deadline (the day of the visit) is not definitely known. Pressure can build to the point of ineffectiveness unless the team leader establishes a planning process with regular check-ups to make sure that the team meets standards on an ongoing basis. The whole team will perform better if stress levels are reduced.

Daniel Goleman's well-known research on emotional intelligence emphasizes how vital it is for leaders to be able to connect emotionally with their followers. He explains in his book *Primal Leadership* that a leader's emotional health is of *primal* (or first) importance to the overall success of the organization. The resonant leader is in sync with his followers and can influence the entire company's emotional tone—either positively or negatively. Goleman describes four domains of emotional intelligence—self-awareness, self-management, social awareness, and relationship management—which are further broken down into 18 competencies. Goleman states that the most effective leaders are those who possess traits in all four domains; however, no one possesses all of the competencies he lists. Goleman also connects the emotional and mental aspects of a leader's health and well-being when he says, "Gifted leadership occurs where heart and head—feeling and thought—meet. These are the two wings that allow a leader to soar."[5]

In *Servant Leadership*, author Robert Greenleaf emphasizes the spiritual aspect of leadership by identifying the essence of leadership as the desire to serve others and fulfill a higher purpose—something beyond ourselves.[6] Joseph Jaworski, who founded the American Leadership Forum according to Greenleaf's principles, focuses on the spiritual aspect of leadership in his book *Synchronicity: The Inner Path of Leadership.* Jaworski stresses the importance of service to others, "Giving our life over to something larger than ourselves, the call to become what we were meant to become—the call to achieve our 'vital design.'"[7] He also discusses how trusting in a force beyond ourselves can create meaningful coincidences in our lives. According to Jaworski, such synchronicities can provide guidance to leaders, especially during difficult times. He also suggests that this is necessary as well for the organization's well-being. Consider a worst-case scenario where a leader dies prematurely, perhaps because he or she ignored obvious warning signs or known risk factors for a particular condition. The most effective leaders are those who regularly tune in to their own inner wisdom and trust in the unseen powers of an interconnected universe.

I have seen firsthand how a leader's failing health can significantly impact his ability to lead. In such a case, the organization can be set back considerably. Key-man insurance can provide some financial protection in this situation, and a good succession plan can position the leader's replacement to take the reins. However, neither the right insurance nor a good plan can restore the leader's energy, vision, and influence, which drove the organization forward.

I worked with an organization in a less extreme case in which a senior manager was known for throwing violent temper tantrums. He had terrorized and intimidated nearly everyone in his division. He was also a very poor communicator who rarely returned phone calls and often sent terse (sometimes one-word only) responses to substantive emails. He also had a habit of failing to show up for meetings that he had called. As I assessed this individual and his workforce, I found his division to be filled with task-doers, who often had little or no initiative or imagination, and whose performance was extremely low. This scenario is an excellent example of the potentially toxic and far-reaching effects that a leader with poor emotional health can have on the people who work for him. Few employees escape unscathed, and performance is significantly affected.

The same holds true if a leader's personal sense of purpose is not in sync with the organization's mission; the performance of both will suffer. One of the search committees with whom I worked back in my headhunting days chose a candidate with a brilliant career in a highly technical field as their chief executive officer (CEO). However, he did not need these technical skills in his new CEO position. Instead, his leadership style—which had worked well in his technology position—was the antithesis of what the new organization needed. He found himself out of sync with the organization's mission, and was out of a job within a couple of years.

I was particularly impressed by the chapter on renewal (Habit 7) in Stephen Covey's famed publication, *The 7 Habits of Highly Effective People*. This chapter emphasizes how crucial it is to balance the physical, mental, emotional, and spiritual parts of one's being.[8] John Gardner also addressed the importance of renewal in leaders and in their organizations and how, without it, organizations stagnate. "Motivation tends to run down. Values decay," he writes.[9]

My literature review confirmed what I had surmised from my consulting experience: Leaders have to be healthy in mind, body, spirit, and emotions to maximize their effectiveness in organizations. Poor health in any of these areas can have a detrimental impact on organizational performance and productivity. Conversely, restoring and balancing all four aspects of a leader's health adds energy to, and helps organizations regain focus and momentum. Transformed leaders can then help restore their organization to optimum performance by addressing the same physical, emotional, mental, and spiritual aspects of the health of their organization by applying the 4-Ps model.

Leaders frequently find themselves under a great deal of stress. They must make tough decisions, inspire their team, and hit financial targets day in and day out. Most people accept the fact that stress takes its toll on health. Certain diseases, such as coronary artery disease, are quite common in high-powered executives who experience stressful situations on a daily basis. If high-powered and high-stress are adjectives that define your life, you may be at risk of suffering a life-threatening event.

Part Two of this book will provide you with some suggestions for improving your personal health while transforming your organization using the 4-Ps model. You can begin your personal healing process by reconnecting with your life's Purpose, personal mission, and core values. You must then determine what it is you are passionate about, and what emotional blocks, if any, limit your effectiveness as a leader. This will permit you to create a vision and plan for your life in your leadership role. Finally, after you've addressed the first three Ps (Purpose, Passion, and Planning) at the personal level, you will probably find that the fourth P (People) has also improved—and that you have fewer physical symptoms that need attention. You will most likely be taking better care of your physical body, and need fewer medications and visits to your physician. Of course, the 5th P, Perseverance, applies to individuals as well as organizations. People can get their weight or blood pressure under control for a while, but only with perseverance can they maintain significant changes for the long haul.

The personal health assessment tool in Appendix A uses the 4-Ps model to determine if any aspect of your health is out of balance and in need of attention. It is not intended to be a comprehensive history, such as one a physician would take during a complete history and physical exam, nor can it serve as a substitute for a detailed intake evaluation that a psychiatrist or psychologist would perform. It is instead intended to provide an overview of the four aspects of your health, and help you determine whether one or more of them needs attention in order to maximize your leadership effectiveness. I recommend that you take the time now to complete this assessment before moving on to the organization health assessment described in the next chapter.

# CHAPTER 3

# The 4 Ps and Organizational Transformation: Assessing Your Organization

*Health is the ability of an organization to align, execute, and renew itself faster than the competition so that it can sustain exceptional performance over time.*

—Scott Keller and Colin Price, *Beyond Performance*

You will find if you Google "organizational health" that many nonphysician organizational development experts have tried to define this term. Some have even gone so far as to create complex ways to evaluate it, as in the case of McKinsey consultants, Keller and Price, quoted previously.[1] But all of these experts seem to agree that an effective, healthy leader is a key ingredient for creating a healthy organization that enjoys lasting success.

As a physician, I look at organizational health in the same way that I look at an individual's health. Since organizations are made up of people, you'll find the same four aspects of health in individuals exist in organizations as well. Now that you have assessed your personal health status, I'll show you how you can use the 4-Ps model to evaluate your organization's health. This will allow you to see what areas of corporate well-being may be out of kilter and hindering potential success.

Remember that the physical aspect of an organization's health includes not only People, but also physical assets such as buildings, equipment, and finances. The mental aspect of organizational health refers to Planning, which requires that you establish a compelling vision and set attainable goals and objectives that help make your organizational vision a reality. The emotional component refers to Passion and esprit de corps in the workplace, while the spiritual aspect speaks to an organization's Purpose, core values, and service to others.

Several well-known authors have discussed these separate elements of the 4-Ps model, but no one has combined all four to give a more complete picture of your organization's well-being and potential for lasting success. For example, William Plamondon, former President and CEO of Budget Rent-a-Car Corporation, discussed the importance of physical energy in both leaders and organizations in *The Leader of the Future*, the Drucker Foundation's collection of leadership essays. Plamondon writes:

*An organization is more than the sum of its people, products, and capital. It's organic. It has a life of its own. If it is to stay healthy and grow, leaders need to keep it open to the environment and attuned to the signals of the market. This ensures that the company and the systems within it stay resilient and organized around company requirements.*[2]

Plamondon is referring to the organization's sense of Purpose when he says that the organization needs to be *in sync* with the marketplace.

In *Primal Leadership*, Daniel Goleman addresses the importance of Passion in a healthy organization when he writes, "Understanding the powerful role of emotions in the workplace sets the best leaders apart from the rest—not just in tangibles such as better business results and the retention of talent, but also in the all-important intangibles, such as higher morale, motivation, and commitment."[3] According to Goleman, the best leaders are those who are able to connect with their followers not only on an intellectual level, but also on an emotional level. I have coached several physician leaders who had difficulty with this. They were brilliant clinicians, but were unable to motivate their team to optimal performance because they lacked the ability to understand how their actions—including impatient outbursts—affected the emotions of their support staff. (Think about Hugh Laurie's character Dr. House from the eponymous television show.) This is why teaching them emotional intelligence skills significantly improved their ability to lead and manage their team.

Creating a compelling vision and a workable strategic plan are other aspects of a healthy organization that Stephen Covey addresses in *First Things First* by saying, "A powerful shared vision has a profound effect on quality of life—in the family, in the organization, in any situation where we work with others."[4] Having a common vision can unite any group of people so that their efforts, be it at work or at play, are cohesive, leading to maximal success.

Again in *Primal Leadership*, Goleman refers to People in a successful organization when he writes that ". . . climate—how people feel about working for a company—can account for 20 to 30 percent of business performance,"[5] There is sound proof to Goleman's claim. In their comprehensive review of 225 academic studies, happiness experts Lyubomirsky, King, and Diener found that happy employees have, on average, 31 percent higher productivity, 37 percent higher sales, and 300 percent higher creativity.[6] In short—it pays (figuratively and literally) to keep your people content.

## Look Beyond the Chief Complaint

When assessing what ails your company, you must do what you do in a patient evaluation and look beyond the chief complaint. Revenues may be down. Morale may be low. Staff turnover rate may be high. Customer complaints or even lawsuits against your company may have increased. Each of these is a potential chief complaint; in other words, the most obvious presenting problem. However, you cannot simply hire a financial consultant, a motivational guru, or a crackerjack corporate attorney and expect to fix the problem. And even if you do, the fix may not last long. Unless you look deeper for the root cause of the chief complaint—as I learned to do when treating patients—the problem will recur, or a new one will arise. It is also critical to develop and consistently use a renewal process that ensures your organization's lasting success.

Of course, all of the 4 Ps are interrelated. For example, if the chief complaint is that revenues are down, people may get laid off, which will likely incite fear and angst among the remaining employees. Morale then sinks, passion in the workplace dwindles, and a decline in customer service follows.

Or perhaps the chief complaint is an aging facility. In this case, there may have been a lack of planning or no clear vision about what infrastructure would be needed in the future. The deteriorating workplace may prompt a drop in morale and present a less than prosperous image to the public, thereby causing sales to decline.

There are a variety of well-known and frequently used organizational assessment tools that can help determine which of the 4 Ps may be most problematic. For example, if the chief complaint seems to involve People, then 360-degree assessments or personality testing may help to delineate the true nature of the problem. If the chief complaint is declining profits, then a financial audit that includes revenue cycle analysis may better clarify the issue you need to address.

If the chief complaint appears to involve Planning, and too much bureaucracy and red tape have caused organizational stagnation or even paralysis, then you can use Lean or Six Sigma techniques to analyze the situation and improve your processes. It's possible to unblock or eliminate logjams using such methods, thereby helping the organization to become more efficient and productive.

Perhaps the board is unaware of current market trends and is not focused on strategically positioning your company for future success as the marketplace changes. A company with this problem would want to use a market survey or environmental scan to educate board members and help them make well-informed decisions about future strategies.

You may be very surprised by what you discover when you look beyond the chief complaint. I was quite taken aback by a situation involving one of my hospital clients, whose medical staff leaders had asked me to help them resolve issues they were having with the hospital administration. I assumed, based on what the physicians had initially told me, that the administration was primarily responsible for the bulk of the problems. But upon looking deeper, I discovered that there was a great deal of misinformation circulating among the medical staff. Communication with the administration had come to a standstill because key medical staff leaders never responded to emails, phone calls, or even certified letters. These same physician leaders would not allow the CEO to attend many of the Medical Executive Committee meetings. It became apparent that some of the physicians were causing some of the problems that needed to be resolved. Therefore, the chief complaint of a poor administration proved to be quite misleading. Only by digging deeper could I get to the root of the problem and begin work to correct the actual problem.

The Joint Commission (TJC), an organization that accredits hospitals, now requires them to institute a process called a root cause analysis whenever a medical error occurs. This process assumes that there is more to the situation than just the initial obvious error, or the chief complaint. It asks the question: What else happened at the system level that caused the error to occur? TJC insists that hospitals dig deeper in order to prevent future errors and improve patient safety. Looking beyond the chief complaint is essential, in fact, life-saving in many cases.

## Lasting Success

According to McKinsey consultants Scott Keller and Colin Price (quoted at the very beginning of this chapter), healthy companies are able to sustain excellence over time. In other words, they produce success that lasts. Keller and Price define a healthy organization as one having the following three traits:

1. "Internal alignment," meaning that the "organization has shared objectives that are supported by its culture and climate and are meaningful to individual employees."

2. "Quality of execution," meaning that the "organization has the capabilities, management processes, and motivation to execute with excellence."

3. The "capacity to renew itself," meaning that "the organization is effective at understanding, interacting with, shaping, and adapting to its situation and external environment."[7]

Not surprisingly, McKinsey data demonstrates that there is a close correlation between performance and health: The healthier the company, the higher the performance. The most successful companies manage not only performance but also health in order to produce long-lasting results.[8]

The 5th P, Perseverance, also plays a key role in creating lasting success and should be an element that companies factor into their renewal process. Chapter 9 will discuss specifically how to do this. It emphasizes how crucial it is for companies to maintain long-term commitment and focus, and build endurance through ongoing renewal, in addition to keeping all 4 Ps in excellent working order, to maximize success on a long-term basis.

The organizational health assessment in Appendix B uses the 4-Ps model as a diagnostic tool to give you an overview of the types of issues that can arise in each of these key areas of your organization's health. It is not meant to provide a definitive diagnosis of what ails your company. Rather, it should simply point you in the direction of what area or areas you need to address and possibly repair in order to guarantee future success.

Some areas might seem to be more problematic than others. Chances are that these are the same areas that are of concern in your personal health assessment. Many things contribute to an organization's overall health and prosperity. However, since you as a leader have direct control over these areas, your personal and your organization's health are likely to mirror each other in this regard. Before moving on to Part Two of this book, which provides treatment suggestions for each of the Ps that might be causing a problem in your organization, I urge you to complete the organizational health assessment so that you know which areas to focus on.

# The Treatment from Inside Out: Transforming Your Organization

# CHAPTER 4

# Realigning Your Organization's Purpose and Core Values

*Affirming purpose and values through service is a regular part of how great companies express their identities.*
—Rosabeth Moss Kanter, *Harvard Business Review*,
November 2011

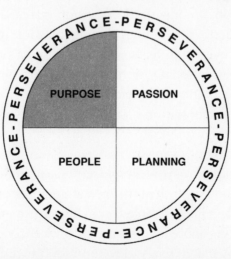

The first step in transforming your organization is to take a good, hard look at your organization's Purpose—the first of the 4 Ps—and core values by answering a few simple questions like: Why are you in business? What business are you in? Is your business in alignment with what your current and potential customers need? Does your purpose serve a higher good? What core values shape your corporate identity? Have either your purpose or core values gotten off track over the years because of inattention to them, or a rapidly changing marketplace?

## Core Purpose: The Mission Statement

An organization's mission statement should define its Purpose, which should be fairly constant; it isn't something that changes from one year to the next. It also should be short and memorable, not consisting of paragraph after paragraph of well-crafted but hard-to-memorize phrases. Your strategic planning team must review it at regular intervals to make sure the company remains true to its purpose and doesn't deviate into uncharted territory. If the marketplace and demand for the company's services has changed, you may need to update the Mission Statement to make sure your purpose aligns with your changing customers' needs.

By comparison, an organization's vision statement must address forward movement. Where does the organization see itself in two, three, five, or even ten years? We will discuss how to create a compelling organizational vision in Chapter 6. But first, there are some important points to consider when reviewing, and possibly realigning, the organization's purpose and subsequently igniting passion within the workforce.

I have read dozens of mission statements in my work and have found them to range from one or two sentences to full paragraphs. As stated earlier, the longer the mission statement, the less memorable it is—and the less likely people throughout the company can para-phrase it, let along quote it verbatim. I always encourage boards that insist on longer versions to also develop a short tagline that everyone throughout the organization can quote and use in marketing materials to succinctly state the organization's reason for being in business.

I have attended several strategic planning retreats during which the review of the mission statement often takes less than 10 or 15 minutes—hardly a long enough period of time. Staying true to your organization's purpose—or reviewing and adapting it to meet changing market forces—are key ingredients in determining future success. It is a serious matter that deserves a longer discussion—not a quick rubber stamp before moving on to other topics.

Some mission statements serve a historical purpose, such as that of the Massachusetts Medical Society. It has one of the oldest medical society mission statements in the United States, dating back to 1781 when the organization was founded, and it states:

> *The purposes of the Massachusetts Medical Society shall be to do all things as may be necessary and appropriate to advance medical knowledge, to develop and maintain the highest professional and ethical standards of medical practice and healthcare, and to promote medical institutions formed on the liberal principles for the health, benefit and welfare of the citizens of the Commonwealth.*

This mission statement has remained relevant even now, although the use of the words "liberal principles" may seem unclear in this day and age. If a historical mission statement remains relevant to this day, it is very important to have a current, forward-looking vision for the organization, as we will discuss in Chapter 6.

I facilitated a strategic planning retreat for the San Francisco Medical Society (SFMS) several years ago. I began by focusing on the organization's mission, which at the time stated the following:

> *The San Francisco Medical Society is a not-for-profit organization advocating the interests of physicians and their patients in the improvement of the public health.*

I discovered prior to the retreat that the organization had wandered off track from its core purpose. It had been raising nondues revenue by renting out its Victorian headquarters and catering events for other businesses and individual parties like weddings and bar mitzvahs. The Executive Director and CEO, Mary Lou Licwinko, had a chef, a sous-chef, and caterers on her staff, in addition to medical society personnel. The proceeds from these events went to support the building costs.

The SFMS Board decided to refocus on its reason to be in business, jettison its noncore business, sell the building, and conduct a Needs Assessment of the physicians in the San Francisco Bay area. Its membership rose, and today its new Mission Statement is posted on its website as follows:

> *The San Francisco Medical Society's primary purpose is to improve the health of all San Franciscans by uniting and supporting the local physician community. The San Francisco Medical Society is a non-profit organization that advocates for physician and patient rights, unites physicians of all specialties to create a solid local medical community, and works to improve the health of all San Franciscans by providing support and education to physicians and patients.*

Ms. Licwinko relates that they sold the building "in the nick of time"—because the need for caterers dropped significantly due to the downturn in the economy shortly after the sale. Had they kept the building, the SFMS would probably not be in business today. Instead, it is a healthy organization with reserves, focused on serving physicians and their patients in the San Francisco Bay area. By aligning its purpose with its current and potential members' needs, the SFMS has prospered—even in a time when many membership organizations have not.

## The Netflix Story: Changing Its Core Purpose

Another example of an organization wandering off purpose is Netflix, the largest company providing online movie rentals for home viewing. Though originally done through the mail, Netflix now provides streaming videos, and has the following mission statement:

> *Our appeal and success are built on providing the most expansive selection of DVDs; an easy way to choose movies; and fast, free delivery.*

However, the company decided to raise its rental fees significantly from $9.99 a month to $15.98 per month in July 2011 as it split off its mail-order service from its streaming video service. This business decision prompted a huge customer outcry, with 800,000 cancelling their service within weeks, and its stock falling by 75 percent.[1] While Netflix CEO Reed Hastings issued a public apology, the new rates did not change. Hastings said in his apology:

> *For the past five years, my greatest fear at Netflix has been that we wouldn't make the leap from success in DVDs to success in streaming. Most companies that are great at something—like AOL dialup or Borders bookstores—do not become great at new things people want (streaming for us).[2]*

In attempting to change its core purpose, Netflix left behind many of its customers who believed that part of Netflix's mission should be the ease and low cost of obtaining DVDs. The Netflix story also demonstrates how difficult it can be for organizations to transition to meet the needs of a rapidly changing marketplace. Netflix does seem to be righting itself now by charting a new direction that focuses on TV streaming in expanded territories, but its ultimate success won't be determined for awhile.[3]

We will discuss the problem of adjusting to market forces later in this chapter as well as in Chapters 6 and 7 about the third P, Planning. I always emphasize the importance of doing an environmental scan at the beginning of any strategic planning process to make sure your business is aligned with the marketplace and can anticipate rapid changes in customers' needs as much as possible.

## Core Values

In her article for the *Harvard Business Review* in November 2011 entitled "How Great Companies Think Differently," Harvard Business School Professor Rosabeth Moss Kanter says that "Purpose and values—not the widgets made—are at the core of an organization's identity, and they can guide people in their efforts to find new widgets that serve society." She goes on to say, "Affirming purpose and values through service is a regular part of how great companies express their identities."[4]

Not only should an organization review its Mission Statement every few years to make sure it is aligned with changing market forces and serves the needs of its customers; it should also review its core values, the principles that help define its culture, how a company operates internally, and how the external world perceives it.

Values provide common ground and can help determine an organization's structure by answering questions like: Is the organizational chart hierarchical or flat? Do people accomplish tasks on teams or as individuals? Values can also determine a company's internal management style and culture. Is it competitive or collaborative? Are leaders transactional or transformational? Is communication open and transparent or provided on only a need-to-know basis? Does the organization value vision and creativity, and encourage ongoing education?

Values should be memorable, just like the mission statements. Some of my clients have even put their values on employee ID badges to serve as a constant reminder of what the organization considers important. Others post the values in public places and on their websites, where employees and customers alike can see them. By maintaining a constant purpose and values that do not change, a company creates an identity that appears coherent both internally and externally.

## Core Values Gone Awry: The Wall Street Debacle

Since the demise of long-standing Wall Street financial services firms such as Lehman Brothers, Bear Stearns, and Merrill Lynch, there have been a lot of analyses conducted about the causes of their fall. Though the information learned could fill numerous books, one key lesson is that those firms' core values shifted as the marketplace shifted. Rather than following traditional investment strategies that had shown proven financial success over many years, they began to embrace aggressiveness, creative investment strategies, and making money quickly for money's sake alone—thereby taking undo risk with clients' portfolios. Greed became a mainstay of the Wall Street culture.

When in business, Lehman Brothers' mission statement included its values and read as follows:

*Our mission is to build unrivaled partnerships with and value for our clients through the knowledge, creativity, and dedication of our people, leading to superior results for our shareholders.*

In business since 1850, Lehman Brothers' stock reached a record high of $86.18 per share in February 2007; by 2008, it was the fourth-largest investment-banking firm in the United States. But during the spectacular week of September 8, 2008, its stock plummeted to being worth only pennies. Lehman Brothers seemed to value creativity to such an extent that it led to a culture of unethical behavior that put clients at risk, and encouraged overly aggressive business practices.[5]

It is interesting to note the Code of Business Conduct and Ethics that appears on the website of multinational conglomerate Berkshire Hathaway, at www.berkshirehathaway.com/govern/ethics.pdf. In the Purpose section of this document, it states the following:

*The Company is proud of the values with which it conducts business. It has and will continue to uphold the highest levels of business ethics and personal integrity in all types of transactions and interactions. To this end, this Code of Business Conduct and Ethics serves to (1) emphasize the Company's commitment to ethics and compliance with the law; (2) set forth basic standards of ethical and legal behavior; (3) provide reporting mechanisms for known or suspected ethical or legal violations; and (4) help prevent and detect wrongdoing.*

Warren Buffett, CEO of Berkshire Hathaway, has been known for many years as a man of integrity who can be trusted in his business dealings. This core value has helped set his company and its many subsidiaries apart in the business world in stark contrast to the Wall Street firms that failed.

## Core Values as Guideposts for Success: The Story of Zappos

On October 28, 2011, reporter Barbara Walters did a *20/20* story about business people who had become billionaires—not the recent Wall Street way, but by the old-fashioned method: doing hard work. One very successful company that she covered in the segment entitled "Billionaire Secrets" was Zappos, an online shoe retailer that provides 24-hour free shipping of over 1,000 brands of shoes. It was sold to Amazon.com in 2009 for $1.2 billion. Walters's story focused on Zappos CEO, Tony Hsieh, who built the company based on a mission of exceptional service and core values that include having fun and being "a little weird."

As Zappos's website states, "We've aligned the entire organization around one mission: to provide the best customer service possible. Internally, we call this our WOW philosophy."[6] The Zappos Family Core Values are prominently listed on its website as follows:

Core Value #1: Deliver WOW Through Service

Core Value #2: Embrace and Drive Change

Core Value #3: Create Fun and a Little Weirdness

Core Value #4: Be Adventurous, Creative, and Open-Minded

Core Value #5: Pursue Growth and Learning

Core Value #6: Build Open and Honest Relationships with Communication

Core Value #7: Build a Positive Team and Family Spirit

Core Value #8: Do More with Less

Core Value #9: Be Passionate and Determined

Core Value #10: Be Humble

Zappos' mission and core values help define a very unique but strong culture, and as Hsieh told Walters, "Companies [that have] strong cultures tend to outperform [those] that don't."[7] According to the *20/20* story, every employee of the company lives and breathes these values. In other words, the company has created a culture of service, fun, creativity, passion, and humility (as stated in the core values), which, in turn, has led to great success for both the CEO and the overall organization.

## Evolving Missions: Assessing Your Market

In order to keep your company true to its mission while simultaneously aligned with market needs, it is important to regularly assess external trends and changing customer demands. One cannot overemphasize the importance of conducting an environmental scan when undergoing a strategic planning process. Only by understanding your marketplace will you be able to adjust your company's vision, goals, and objectives accordingly. Though these may change frequently to address market concerns (as we will discuss in Chapter 6 and Chapter 7), your company's purpose and core values—your corporate identity—should not be easily susceptible to the winds of change.

Very few leaders have the kind of vision that Steve Jobs had—vision that enabled him to predict what his customers and potential customers would want before *they* were even aware of what they wanted. Most leaders need to get enough market information and customer feedback prior to taking their organization in a new direction. Otherwise, they run the risk being out of sync with their customers' needs and may end up in no-man's-land where sales decline because they're providing something that's suboptimal or no longer needed.

Missions can change over time. It is still advisable to take a measured approach to corporate evolution based on industry knowledge. However, new technologies are disrupting whole industries and forcing some companies to evolve dramatically—or even go out of business. An obvious example is the bookstore chain Borders, which did not evolve fast enough as the digital age hit the book industry. In contrast, competitor Barnes & Noble kept up with digital books by creating its own tablet book reader, the Nook, and has remained an important player in the retail book-selling business.

It is informative to compare and contrast these two competitors' mission statements. Both profess a commitment to external and internal customer service; however, one can notice subtle differences between the two. The Barnes & Noble mission statement begins: *"Our mission is to operate the best specialty retail business in America, regardless of the product we sell . . . ."*

It goes on to state that the product they sell is books, but there is a certain flexibility to what they sell in that opening sentence. It also says, *"We will continue to bring our industry nuances of style and approaches to bookselling which are consistent with our evolving aspirations."*

This statement indicates the company's forward thinking and desire to evolve as part of its core purpose.

By comparison, Borders's mission statement starts out by stating a much closer link to actual products: *"To be the best loved provider of books, music, movies, and other entertainment and informational products and services . . . ."*

Although the company lists "innovation" in the mission statement and also as one of its "supporting attributes," it also lists "ambiance" for book browsing in both, an indication of a more fixed, in-store approach to book-selling than its competitor—one that ultimately led to its downfall.

## Personal Mission Statements

It can be helpful for leaders of organizations to develop personal mission statements that reflect their core values. A personal mission statement might answer questions like: Why are you on this planet? What are you meant to do with your life? What do you value most? There are several how-to books and workshops to guide you through this process. After leaving Malibu, I attended one of those workshops, given by a Stephen Covey 7 Habits trainer, where I developed a personal mission statement that has served me well to this day. It is very simple, memorable, and reads:

"I am a healer and a teacher."

My core values include:

Integrity and Fairness
Knowledge and Education
Kindness and Compassion
Creativity and Innovation
Family and Life Balance
Fun!

My mission statement and core values have helped me make multiple strategic business decisions over the years. I have built a teaching institute that helps physicians become better leaders so that they can provide better care for their patients. I coach physician leaders, healthcare executives, and difficult doctors. My company, The Institute for Medical Leadership, has the following mission statement:

> *To teach leadership skills and provide executive coaching to physician leaders and healthcare executives so that they develop innovative, collaborative, patient-centered solutions to today's challenges that will transform not only their institutions but ultimately the healthcare delivery system as a whole.*

At times when I have taken on assignments that have proven to be more difficult than anticipated, my mission statement has led me to reevaluate the project by prompting me to question whether I'm being true to my core purpose and values. If the challenge fits with my purpose, then I keep going. If I find that I'm not longer in sync with my core values, then I readjust and focus on what I believe I should be doing.

Personal mission statements can evolve over time, just like organizational mission statements. I've recently added, "I am a writer," to my own mission statement, as writing has become a regular part of my work. It now is apparent that this is something I am meant to be doing in addition to public speaking, coaching, and putting on educational conferences.

## Changes in the Healthcare Industry

The healthcare industry is changing radically nowadays, due to technological advances and payment reform. Linking physicians' payment from Medicare and other payors to clinical outcomes data is forcing consolidation in the industry.

As President of the Los Angeles County Medical Association's Bay District 5 (a district stretching from Malibu to LAX along the coast), I conducted several focus groups with doctors in solo or small group practices in Los Angeles' Westside. I also conducted a focus group with Permanente physicians at Kaiser's West Los Angeles facility.

There was a huge difference in the responses I received from these groups. The solo and small group practice physicians were experiencing a great deal of anger and fear about what lies ahead. Some were quite miserable, waiting for the sword of Damocles to fall. On the other hand, the Permanente doctors used words like "happy," and "optimistic," and conveyed that they were "enjoying" their practices. They did not have to worry about managing a practice on a daily basis and were free to focus exclusively on delivering the best patient care possible.

Such a disparity begs the question: What is the purpose of being a physician in clinical practice? Is it to deliver optimal patient care? Or is it to be a small business owner while also providing medical care? It has been the latter in the cottage industry of American medicine for more than a century. Though physicians saw patients, of course, they were also small-business owners—who often had little business training, experience, or innate ability to be successful as such.

Physicians all over the country are now grappling with this issue. Hospitals are employing more and more physicians in all states where it is legal to do so. Younger doctors want jobs in order to pay off staggering medical school debt. The old guard still wants to hang on and practice medicine the way they have in the past, either on their own or in a two- or three-person group.

I have noticed that once physicians bite the bullet and merge their practice or join an employed physician group, many of them work through the discomfort of change relatively quickly. They have fewer administrative hassles, are less angry and fearful, and sleep better at night. They become much happier since they can devote their time to aligning with their true core purpose: delivering quality patient care.

There are some physicians experiencing considerable distress as the healthcare world changes around them. I recommend that these doctors assess their purpose and core values. Are they meant to provide the best possible quality medical care that they can? Are they meant to be small-business owners? Are they meant to be both? They may find that patient care is truly what they do best, what they love to do, and therefore what they are meant to be doing. Although some physicians—myself included—will always be entrepreneurs, honestly evaluating themselves may open their eyes. They might find the hassles of being a small-business owner unnecessary; they may be able to find a better way to provide quality patient care in a different practice setting.

As with the healthcare industry and physicians, professionals in other industries that are undergoing significant rapid change will find it beneficial to evaluate their own sense of purpose and their core values, and then decide what business or career decisions are most appropriate.

Before moving on to ignite the second P, Passion, in your organization, please review the following prescription for success—an action plan which summarizes the key points in this chapter.

## The Prescription: Purpose and Core Values

1. Begin transforming your organization by analyzing if your company is staying true to its purpose and core values.

2. Reassess the marketplace to determine if your organization is still meeting your customers' needs.

3. Do an internal evaluation to determine if values have drifted and core identity has suffered.

4. As a leader, develop a personal mission statement and a list of your own core values. Determine if you are being true to your own purpose and core values in your current position and in the direction you are leading your company.

5. Make any needed adjustments, working with your leadership team if you need to rewrite your organization's mission statement.

6. Realign your organization with its core values, if necessary.

7. Rethink your career if your personal purpose and core values are out of sync with your organization.

# CHAPTER 5

# Restoring Passion in the Workplace

*We may affirm absolutely that nothing great in the world has been accomplished without passion.*

—Georg Wilhelm Friedrich Hegel,
*Philosophy of History*

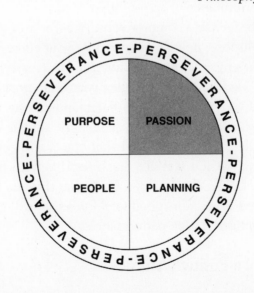

Achieving organizational success through quality leadership involves more than just great ideas, winning strategies, and being true to your purpose and core values. A sense of passion— or a depth of feeling and emotion—must drive the organization forward. As Daniel Goleman expressed in his renowned book *Emotional Intelligence*, the most effective leaders connect with their followers' hearts *and* minds—that is, with both thoughts and feelings.[1] Passion is a great motivator, and a necessary element of success in business.

There are several key strategies for motivating your workforce. Leaders must first be motivators. So if they are not passionate or at least enthusiastic about the company's purpose, they're unlikely to inspire anyone to follow them. Employees may do what is expected of them, but only because they are paid or receive some company benefit. If their bonus or an extra perk depends on their productivity, they will most likely do the minimum required to get the reward. But will they give it their all? Unless they, too, feel passion for their work, their efforts will be suboptimal.

Think about what would compel you to give your organization your peak performance. Factors other than having an inspiring leader might be feeling a common sense of purpose or empowerment to work on solutions; being recognized for your efforts; or doing fun work that you enjoy with a quality team of people. All of these make it more likely that you will give your best effort.

However, if you have a difficult or demanding boss who criticizes unfairly and micromanages, or if you lack the time or resources you need to complete projects, or feel that your efforts are unappreciated or ignored—then you are much less likely to perform at an optimal level. Leaders have to recognize that they are key factors in developing a passionate, inspired workforce that will give their best effort and function at peak performance.

## The Effect of a Positive Attitude

Both individuals and organizations have long debated about how to ignite passion and eliminate negative emotions. Some experts advocate for the power of positive thinking: If you change your attitude, you can change your life and your organization. Dr. Norman Vincent Peale first introduced this concept in his classic 1952 book entitled *The Power of Positive Thinking*—a publication that has helped to reshape millions of lives. Dr. Peale tells the story of a television talk show host who asked an old man what the secret to happiness was. The old man answered that every morning he got up and had two choices for the day: either to be happy or not to be happy. He simply always chose to be happy.[2]

While this approach may seem far too simplistic to some, the power of a positive attitude and positive emotions has been proven time and time again. Every single day, each of us faces the same choice as the old man in Dr. Peale's book. We can choose to let ourselves be consumed by negative thoughts and emotions, or we can change our attitude and allow positive thoughts and emotions to rule the day.

I was surprised, but quite impressed, by a group of nurse managers at a hospital where I was serving as Interim Chief Medical Officer while on a six-month assignment to initiate a hospital-wide cultural change. The nurses had been dealing with disruptive physician behavior; some of the doctors had yelled at, berated, and demeaned them repeatedly for many years. There was an atmosphere of fear and intimidation throughout the hospital. Needless to say, morale among the nursing staff had suffered greatly.

Part way through my term, I decided to give each nursing unit a framed motivational poster from Successories, a motivational products and awards company. I gave each nurse manager a choice of three different themes: Excellence, Service, or Attitude. I thought most of them would choose the Excellence poster, but they overwhelmingly chose the Attitude poster, which had a picture of a lightning bolt and the following quote:

> *"Our lives are not determined by what happens to us, but by how we react to what happens; not by what life brings to us, but by the attitude we bring to life. A positive attitude causes a chain reaction of positive thoughts, events and outcomes. It is a catalyst . . . a spark that creates extraordinary results."*[3]

This poster's message is simple: A positive attitude spreads quickly and ignites passion throughout an organization. The nurse managers knew it would take time for the physicians to change their bad behavior, even with the new hospital code of conduct policy I developed. However, they thought—correctly—that changing their own reactions to the unwanted behavior and keeping a positive attitude would speed the process and create a much more positive work environment.

## The Effect of Negative Emotions

Leaders must not only inspire and motivate their followers; they must also clear away any negative feelings or emotional blocks that may limit their organization's success. Once you deal with these hindrances, it is easier to begin the planning process. An organization's vision and goals and objectives will be much stronger if a leader has ignited passion throughout the company and has minimized—or even eliminated—negative, destructive energy.

Scores of leaders have been trained to suppress their emotions at all costs, and showing emotion is considered a sign of weakness in many business situations. But this kind of unexpressed negative emotions can severely impact a leader's ability, and can keep his or her followers from performing optimally. Negative emotions that build up over time and remain hidden can hamper creativity, cause a breakdown in communication, and limit an organization's goals and objectives.

Scientific studies have shown that people have more heart attacks on Monday mornings, perhaps triggered by the fear and anxiety of having to face a new week at a stressful job.[4] Deaths peak the day after Christmas among Christians, and the day after the Chinese New Year among Chinese people—both emotionally laden times of the year for each culture.[5] On the flip side, the burgeoning field of happiness research, discussed in depth in the January/February 2012 issue of the *Harvard Business Review*, has shown that happy employees have a 31 percent higher productivity rate.[6]

Some experts advocate for a cathartic release of negative emotions in order to clear them. This can be hard to do in a corporate setting; however, we have to acknowledge the 800-pound gorilla of negativity in the room rather than ignore it. Leaders and followers must deal with problems that trigger pent-up negative tension before the organization can maximize its success.

## The Biochemistry of Emotion

It's helpful to understand a little about the biochemistry of emotions in order to strengthen positive feelings and diffuse negative ones throughout your company. In her fascinating book, *Molecules of Emotion*, former Chief of the Brain Biochemistry Section at the National Institute of Mental Health (NIMH) and Professor of Physiology and Biophysics at Georgetown University, Dr. Candice Pert, describes how emotions have dramatic effects on our physiology at the molecular level—and how changing negative feelings to positive ones can actually heal us.[7]

At the NIMH, Dr. Pert studied neuropeptides and their receptors in the brain, which she called "peptides with an attitude." She discovered the opiate receptor in brain tissue, which led to the discovery of endorphins, the morphine-like, mood-elevating, pain-relieving peptides that occur naturally in our bodies. Many other peptides of emotion and their receptors have been discovered since her original finding; in fact, it's possible that there is one for each emotion that we experience.

These peptides of emotion have been found not only in the brain, but also in the immune, endocrine, and gastrointestinal systems. Dr. Pert and her colleagues proposed that these peptides and their receptors form a two-way information network that connects these systems throughout the body. As these peptides of emotion bind with their receptors on cell surfaces in different organs, chemical and vibratory energy changes occur throughout the system as we experience different emotions.

Dr. Pert's work has demonstrated how emotions can change both our physiology and our health status at the molecular level. This applies to group situations where other individuals can feel one person's emotions—either positive or negative—and they spread throughout the group. And because the Law of Attraction states that like vibrational energy tends to attract like vibrational energy, positive people tend to attract positive people into their lives, while negative people tend to attract other negative people.[8] In this way, one team member's emotions can impact the entire team's energy level and productivity.

## Releasing Negative Emotions

Now that you know that emotions affect human biochemistry, we can look at which emotions are blocking your organization. The specific treatment and organizational transformation will depend on which emotions are churning away under the surface of the organization's "business as usual" appearance.

Three of the most common emotional blocks in today's difficult economy are boredom, anger, and fear. People may feel stuck in dead-end jobs as the national unemployment rate rose to 9.1 percent in 2011.[9] They may be angry about not receiving a promotion they think they deserve, but know that opportunities elsewhere are lacking. And whether they're happy or not in their current position, they may be afraid of being downsized and out of a job—*any* job—and losing their health insurance, and possibly even their home and way of life. What follows are some suggestions for dealing with the variety and levels of negative emotions that may be limiting your company's potential success.

### Dealing with Boredom

One key strategy for dealing with boredom in your workforce is to make sure that you have maximized your employees' strengths and covered their weaknesses with other members of the team. We'll cover the concept of putting the right people in the right positions in depth in Chapter 8, which is about developing people. However, it is obviously an important topic to touch on when figuring out how to ignite passion. If you have the right people on your team but have them in the wrong roles—positions for which they are not naturally suited and/or have little interest—they will never function at peak performance. Even if you provide additional training, it is "just not their thing."

One strategy to fight boredom is to make the work fun in some way—perhaps by having a team challenge or a celebration after completing a project. For example, I was surprised on my first day at Heidrick & Struggles by the company mission statement, printed on a paperweight on my desk. It listed eight points, with the eighth being "Have fun." As a physician who had completed arduous training and who spent years as CEO of an emergency medical center dealing with life-and-death decisions on a regular basis, "fun" was not a frequent word in my vocabulary. It seemed odd to me to put it in a mission statement. I wasn't really sure what they even meant!

However, I figured it out soon enough when I was invited to go on a cruise to Mexico with the California consultants. *That* was fun! Then I was invited to Paris for a week for New Search Consultant Orientation with my colleagues from around the world. That was even *more* fun. I started to get the hang of what they meant, and to appreciate the positive spirit that this sense of fun spread throughout the company.

Of course, not every company can send people on cruises or to Paris; however, there are certainly other things you can do for your employees on a much smaller scale. Perhaps you surprise your team with pizza or Chinese food for lunch. Perhaps you have a 5-K race, a *Jeopardy!*-style challenge, or a pumpkin-carving contest with prizes like Starbucks cards or restaurant coupons. One of my clients said that bowling night was a great motivator to develop team spirit and cooperation in her rural community, while tickets to see the Lakers might work better in Los Angeles. Whatever the location or environment, each organization will have different ideas for what would be fun, motivating, and teambuilding for its employees. And remember that getting fun rewards ideas from your workforce can be a motivator in and of itself.

## Resolving Anger

If there is an undercurrent of anger in your organization—whether it's between labor and management, between silos, at board actions, or about restructuring—you must adopt conflict resolution strategies to make sure the organization can maximize its success. We know from psychological studies that anger left unchecked builds—just like a wildfire left unattended. Each mean comment that you hurl at your perceived enemy only incites an equally or even more piercing comment. This, in turn, prompts you to send back an even greater barrage of negative comments, resulting in growing discord. You may get angrier and shoot back more verbal bullets, or perhaps even strike out physically. When anger builds to a crescendo in this manner, resentment sets in, and it is very difficult to escape this vicious cycle. The only way out is to put your anger in check with a clear-cut conflict-resolution strategy that interrupts the inflammatory pattern of discord.

Time and distance are frequently your allies in resolving conflict. You may simply need a cooling-off period to get away from your adversary and gain some perspective on the situation. It can also help quell your anger to realize that your anger hurts *you* more than your intended target. Or you may need to distance yourself from certain friends or colleagues whose negative comments only add fuel to the fire.

You might need to separate the disagreeing parties when resolving serious conflicts, while having a neutral third party—a mediator—intervene. Resolving conflict successfully requires that you distinguish the individuals' personalities from the actual problem, and to aim for win-win solutions that allow each side to get as much of what they want as possible. A mediator can help both sides find common goals; if none exist, he or she can identify which higher goals both aspire to achieve. The mediator can also help each side see new perspectives on the problems and uncover possible solutions while working out the gives and gets, the trade-offs, and the "must-have" deal points in the negotiation.

Forgiveness can certainly help resolve conflicts, but is a strategy that is often forgotten in the heat of battle. We are all human, and we all make mistakes. Yet despite our human weaknesses, most of us do not practice forgiveness when we find ourselves in conflict. We tend toward the "eye-for-an-eye" maxim to which many people adhere. Ironically and sadly, we could resolve our disputes much more easily by making forgiveness part of the resolution process as well.

Another important principle to remember when dealing with anger is one I found in the writings of Dale Carnegie (*How to Win Friends and Influence People*).[10] Carnegie maintains that if you ever have to make the choice between being right and being kind, you should always choose being kind. Yet few people practice this concept in our society. We want to win at any cost, forgetting that conflicts are much easier to resolve when we let kindness and forgiveness guide the process.

## Dispelling Fear

If your workforce seems overcome by fear, a key strategy is to communicate as openly as possible on a regular basis. Fear of the unknown can be overwhelming; it has the power to paralyze employees and destroy their productivity. In his book *Leading Change*, John Kotter emphasizes that leaders must communicate their organization's new change vision repeatedly, using every available method, so that everyone knows in which direction the company is headed.[11] The more transparency there is, the less fear there will be.

Another way to dispel fear is to manage transitions effectively. Loss occurs anytime a company reorganizes. Employees may feel a sense of relief that they still have a job, or optimistic about new opportunities the change has created, but more often they experience anger, sadness, and fear as structures, reporting relationships, and co-workers change.

It can be quite stressful when this kind of transformation takes place throughout an organization. According to William Bridges' classic work *Transitions*, three stages exist in any transition.[12] (See Figure 5.1.) The first stage requires that you face the loss at hand. People must deal with a cycle of emotions during this highly emotional phase, beginning with shock, followed by denial; then anger, sadness, and grief; depression, apathy, or detachment; then shock and denial all over again. This cycle will repeat itself until you break it by accepting the loss. This acceptance then makes it possible for you to move on to the second phase of the transition.

The first phase can induce overpowering depression that may cause employees to lose interest in their work and in life, thereby limiting their performance and productivity. Depression is far more common than most are aware; in fact, according to the National Institute of Mental Health, the prevalence of depression in the United States ranges between 5 and 10 percent of all adult Americans, with women being nearly twice as susceptible as men.[13]

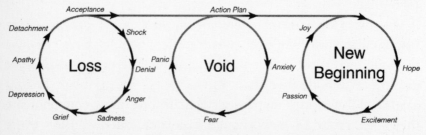

Figure 5.1   The Three Phases of Transition

Greenberg et al. estimated that the annual cost of depressive illness was $83 billion in 2003, an amount that is most likely higher today.[14] Depression can be triggered by a variety of things, including significant loss, news of a life-threatening illness, or as a reaction to grief or to anger. Many therapists believe that it comes as a result of unresolved anger turned inward (yet another good reason to resolve your anger in appropriate ways before it eats away at you).

Some people get stuck in depression, so it's good news that we can effectively treat this affliction. The advent of new pharmaceutical therapies allows the chemical imbalance in the brain that causes the depressive symptoms to be corrected.

Letting go of the past is a very important part of moving through *any* transition. The sooner we let go of things that carry negative energy, the sooner we can clear the way for more positive experiences and interactions to show up in our lives.

Letting go means accepting what has happened and feeling free to move on to the Phase 2 of transition, which I call "the void" and Bridges calls "the neutral zone." Fear is the predominant emotion in this phase. Though you've faced and accepted your loss, you do not know what's coming next. This fear of the unknown causes many people to panic.

A far better choice is to view this second phase of transition as a blank slate upon which you can create anything you want for you and your organization's future. This phase can be a highly creative time if you allow it to be. Imagine you have been given an empty canvas and all the colors of the rainbow with which to paint. What picture of your work and your organization's future would you paint? Overcoming fear in this phase involves remaining calm and tapping into your inner intelligence. We will describe this process in more detail in Chapter 6 when we discuss how to create a compelling vision for your organization.

You will continue in the cyclical second phase of transition until you create an action plan that gets you to a new beginning in Phase 3. Here, you actively engage in external, strategic activities that allow a bright new beginning to take shape. You will successfully create new ideas, connect with new resources, and experience hope, excitement, passion, and joy that lead to growth and prosperity—but only if you have successfully handled the emotions that arose in both Phase 1 (the loss) and Phase 2 (the void).

## Recognizing Burnout

Employees who feel overwhelmed by emotions and fail to deal with them effectively can eventually experience burnout. They feel exhausted and cynical, become sick and tired of their jobs, and are completely devoid of passion. Burnout can afflict anyone, and even high-achieving leaders with big plans for their organization are susceptible to its insidious symptoms. You must take a serious look at your own level of enthusiasm for your work and your organization to determine if you or your employees are at risk or are already burned out. Do you care passionately about what you are doing, and your company's mission and vision? If not, ask yourself if any of the negative emotions described earlier are limiting your enthusiasm and need to be cleared. And remember: only passionate leaders can *truly* inspire their team to follow them and give their best effort.

## The Power of Positive Emotions

So far, we have focused on clearing negative emotions that can block your organization's success. We also need to consider how *positive* emotions can impact your ability to lead your organization. Positive emotions such as joy, love, and compassion can be great healing forces in both your personal life and your organization. A leader's positive attitude will radiate throughout an organization, allowing your followers to experience its motivating effects.

Joy builds into a crescendo in the same way that anger does. You must therefore choose which pattern to follow. Do you want your life to be filled with ever-increasing boredom, anger, and fear? Or would you prefer joy, love, and compassion to continually increase in intensity? The answer is obvious; all of us would much prefer to be happy, filled with positive emotions. But is this as simple as it sounds? Can we just *choose* to shift our emotions and feel better?

The following story demonstrates what I have found to be true in my life over and over again: that I can let go of negative emotions quickly simply by choosing to bring a positive attitude and a sense of humor back into my life. Several years ago while working as a leadership development consultant for a major client, I was surprised and disappointed when the company canceled my contract suddenly without notice because an internal project took precedence. I felt hurt, angry, and sad over the loss, and these emotions occurred almost simultaneously. My young son found me upset in my home office that evening, and decided that the cure for my emotional ills was to watch one of his favorite TV shows, *Whose Line is it Anyway?*.

*Whose Line* was an improvisational show hosted by Drew Carey, which featured skits by world-class comedians. I had never really paid much attention to the show before that evening. But my son pulled out futons for us to sit on and even made microwave popcorn. He was totally intent on doing anything he could to improve my mood and outlook.

As the show started, I was definitely not feeling my upbeat self. Yet after the first five minutes or so, I found myself drawn into the comedic acts. I was laughing at one of the jokes and then another. Soon I was completely immersed in the improvisations, and my work situation had faded completely out of my conscious mind.

By the end of the first half-hour show, my son and I were laughing uproariously, and I was happy to know that there was another half-hour episode of the show on next. My troubles seemed very far away by the end of the second half-hour. They had decreased in their enormity and no longer overwhelmed me. Simply watching the show had interrupted my negative thought patterns and the emotions accompanying them. It gave me the chance to choose laughter over anger and sadness. And the most important thing about this solution was that it worked very quickly.

*Saturday Review* editor Norman Cousins demonstrated the potent healing effect of laughter in his 1991 groundbreaking book, *Anatomy of an Illness as Perceived by the Patient*.[15] Diagnosed with a chronic debilitating illness, ankylosing spondylitis, Cousins found that the sterile, high-tech, hospital environment was not conducive to healing and that his medication regimen was fraught with toxic side effects. He and his physician decided on a course of therapy that included high-dose vitamin C to treat the inflammatory process of the disease and high doses of laughter to boost his immune system. Cousins discovered after watching *Candid Camera* episodes and Marx Brothers' movies that a mere 10 minutes of laughter gave him 2 hours of pain-free sleep. He managed to slowly reverse his illness, much to the surprise of the medical establishment.

Cousins called laughter "internal jogging," believing that it gave the body a therapeutic workout that sent healing emotions throughout its system. And this assertion isn't so far from the truth. The muscles in our face, chest, and abdomen get a mini-workout when we laugh. After we're done, these muscles—including the heart—relax. The relaxation response may last up to 45 minutes, a time during which the blood pressure and the pulse rate decrease. Since anxiety and relaxation cannot co-exist, laughter can block the ill effects that negative emotions have on your physiology.

The Internet has certainly helped spread Cousins' message that "laughter is the best medicine." When I searched that phrase on the web while writing this chapter, I found 4,450,000 sites to visit. Though I couldn't cover all of them, a great number of these sites boasted the theme of healing through positive thoughts and emotions. I found myself laughing wholeheartedly at the online jokes, transforming not only my thoughts and feelings but also my physiology. I felt my entire body relax. The pain in my upper back that I get when working long hours at my computer was completely gone!

# The Power of Caring

My son's efforts to cheer me when we watched *Whose Line is it Anyway?* were in part therapeutic because they made me laugh. He also helped alter my mood because of another powerful emotion at work that night: caring. My son showed great concern for me, and also gave me hugs, which are known to have significant healing benefits.[16]

While this kind of affection isn't appropriate in the workplace, a leader's ability to show that he or she cares about employees can motivate and inspire them. In *Primal Leadership*, author Daniel Goleman lists six types of leadership styles in order of effectiveness. The first four styles—Visionary, Coaching, Affiliative, and Democratic—all include a component of concern for the workforce and are deemed to be positive leadership styles. Two styles, Pacesetting and Commanding, are more authoritative and demanding in their approach to motivating employees and are considered to be negative leadership styles.[17]

I've seen many physician leaders in my coaching career who have identified their own leadership style most closely with Goleman's Pacesetting style, one in which highly trained leaders who set high expectations for themselves also set very high expectations for their teams. Unfortunately, these leaders often find themselves too far ahead of their followers; and their followers often become angry, lose motivation, and lack passion when leaders become too demanding. The more positive leadership styles consider how followers feel and demonstrate a caring approach to motivating the workforce. In short, followers feel valued, as though their thoughts and feelings matter to their leader—because they *do*.

# Passion in the Workplace

Passion in the workplace begins with the leader. We have discussed in this chapter that choosing to adopt a positive attitude can help rid you of negative emotions, rekindle the fire within you, and reconnect you with a sense of excitement for your work. By substituting motivating positive emotions for destructive negative ones, you clear the way for this passion to ignite inside of you.

It may be helpful to make a list of the things in life about which you are passionate, since this isn't always something we keep top-of-mind. Is there something that used to be a lot of fun when you were younger—something you may have forgotten until you dealt with your negative emotions? Perhaps you've repressed certain rewarding experiences because you have felt so overwhelmed by your current responsibilities. Creating this list will help you tap into your inner source of positive energy. And ignited passion is infectious; others will catch your enthusiasm and feel inspired by you. It will become much easier to create and communicate a vision for your organization, motivating others to follow your lead.

After I've clarified the Purpose stage of the 4 Ps during strategic planning retreats that I have conducted for my clients, I then ask attendees to tell the group what they care passionately about in their organization. Why are they working for that company? Is there an issue that the association is addressing or needs to address that particularly stimulates them?

I then use the following exercise at the retreat to clear out negative emotions: I give all retreat attendees identical pieces of paper and identical pens, and ask them to write down what is bothering them about their organization. Then, as the facilitator, I collect the pieces of paper (which are kept anonymous) and tally them on a flip chart. This exercise results in a number of responses, ranging from very few complaints (a good sign) to a laundry list of company ills (clearly more troubling.)

A pattern usually emerges with one or two issues showing up on several pieces of papers. For example, I learned in advance of working with a medical society with a board of twenty physicians that leaders were very pleased to have recruited four women to serve on the board. However, I saw when I collected the anonymous pieces of paper that seven out of twenty attendees had written down "old boys club." In other words, although women were on the board, they had not been integrated into the decision-making structure and felt they were treated as token board members.

Issues that employees write down repeatedly need to be addressed immediately. Bringing the problems to light in this anonymous manner allows leaders to focus attention on them and begin the transformation process. The 800-pound gorilla is no longer buried— and leaders must address it before they can launch any strategic planning efforts that will maximize organizational success.

The next two chapters will examine the third P of strategic transformation: Planning. The first part of planning, discussed in Chapter 6, is to create a compelling vision for your organization. The second part, which I cover in Chapter 7, is about setting realistic goals and objectives so that the compelling organizational vision becomes a reality.

I always urge my clients to make sure that their organization's purpose is aligned with the marketplace and that they've ignited passion throughout the company to the greatest extent possible before diving into Planning. This is the only way they can create a great vision along with an effective plan of action. The following prescription for success will help assure that you have restored passion in the workplace before you move on.

## The Prescription: Passion

1. Identify the things your company is doing in the areas about which you are most passionate.

2. Make a list of the things that bother you the most about your organization.

3. Identify the negative feelings (boredom, anger, fear, etc.) you have about each item on the list you created in step 2.

4. Use processes in this chapter to let go of any negative feelings identified in step 3.

5. Ask each member of your leadership team to do steps 1 through 4 anonymously. Tally the results to see what the group is most passionate about and if any negatives are repeated and clearly of concern to the majority on your leadership team.

6. Address any negatives identified in step 5 before moving on to the Planning process.

# Creating and Communicating a Compelling Organizational Vision

*For something great to happen, there must be a great dream.*
—Robert Greenleaf, *Servant Leadership*

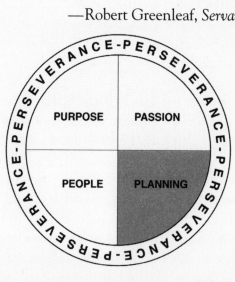

Once you've reevaluated your organization's Purpose and core values and cleared away any Passion-limiting emotional blocks, you can begin the Planning process. You must base your planning on knowledge of the industry, including an analysis of future trends. It is therefore essential to conduct an environmental scan at the onset of this process.

Planning requires that you create a vision based on market trends, and then set goals and objectives to make that vision a reality. Leaders cannot plan everything by themselves. They must be able to work with a team of people to communicate their vision to others in a way that inspires them to follow their lead and set reachable goals that will lead to the company's future success.

This chapter will therefore focus on how to generate this compelling vision and then express it effectively throughout your organization. Chapter 7 will then address how to develop inspiring goals and objectives for your company that motivates your employees to achieve that vision.

The Reverend Martin Luther King, Jr. was an inspiring leader who had a compelling vision for the future of black people in the United States. As many people are aware, he passionately communicated this vision in his "I Have a Dream" speech, which he delivered to more than 250,000 people from the steps of the Lincoln Memorial on August 28, 1963. One of the most memorable quotes from that speech is:

*"I have a dream that my four little children will one day live in a nation where they will not be judged by the color of their skin but by the content of their character. I have a dream today!"*

Dr. King's vision of a color-blind nation inspired a generation of young people to fight for civil rights in this country. He had the ability to visualize a transformed nation in the future, and to communicate that vision using eloquent words to motivate his followers.

Of course, not everyone can be as inspirational as Dr. King; however, I hope that by the end of this chapter, many of you will further expand your right-brain thinking to become more imaginative leaders and to better communicate your vision throughout your organization. Leaders who make an effort to conceive of new ideas and improve their communication skills are better able to introduce innovation and success into their organizations.

## The Importance of Vision in an Organization

Vision in an organization implies action. It should not be stagnant or fixed; rather, it must motivate people to move the company forward. On the other hand, mission or purpose (described in Chapter 4) is more static and should *not* change dramatically from year to year.

The importance of organizational vision became very apparent to me in my first year at consulting firm Heidrick & Struggles. I began working with three senior MBA students at UCLA's Anderson School of Management who conducted a field study about physician executive success factors.[1] They had surveyed 1,229 physician executives in California for the study, 30 percent of whom responded—quite a surprising number for a group of busy doctors.

The study showed that the number-one factor in determining how successfully these physician executives achieved goals for their organization was "building trust." "Vision," on the other hand, was number ten on the list of success factors, while "motivating other people" was number nine.

The fact that trust was number one on the list wasn't entirely unexpected. Physician executives no longer wear white coats or scrubs or carry stethoscopes; they are removed from clinical care these days and instead now have to relate to the business world. Their clinical colleagues often don't view them as real doctors anymore, and might even think they have defected to "the dark side"—hospital administration. Yet the C-suite hospital executives don't consider their physician counterparts to be *real* executives, either. As a result of these divergent perceptions, physician executives frequently find themselves caught in the middle, which only makes it more difficult to get people to trust them. The most successful physician executives turned out to be those who maintained strong trusting relationships with their clinical colleagues while building new trusting relationships with administrators.

The low rankings of both vision and motivating other people were a big surprise to my headhunter colleagues—that is, until we analyzed the responses by job title. Twelve percent of the physician executives had the title of CEO, and these individuals ranked vision as their top success factor, followed by leadership and communication skills, teamwork and creativity, and management experience. These factors seemed much more typical for leaders in any industry.

The students also surveyed doctors who were serving as Senior Vice Presidents (the next step down from the CEOs) in hospitals or health systems, managed care organizations, or insurance companies. These doctors worked in very senior positions where they earned commensurate high salaries, but considered only their clinical background, communication, teamwork, and information management to be their success factors. "Vision" did not even make the list. It became apparent upon further analysis that these physician executives held staff positions; since they had few or no people to manage and motivate, they didn't see vision as important to their success.

This study's results prompted me to find out whether it was possible to teach and develop visioning ability. Perhaps if physicians could learn to be more innovative and visionary—and figure out how to communicate that vision—they might be able to better position themselves as leaders of their organizations as well as in the national healthcare debate.

I sought advice from Dr. David Bresler, a co-founder of The Academy for Guided Imagery. I knew that Dr. Bresler had trained Disney's engineers—called Imagineers—to be more out-of-the-box thinkers, so I invited him to join me at the California Medical Association's Annual Leadership Academy to try to do the same for doctors. He helped me by conducting a workshop on the visioning process, which included guided imagery techniques and proved to be highly effective and well received. I decided to learn some of Dr. Bresler's visualization methods myself, and since then have included guided imagery exercises in some of my leadership workshops.

## Where Does Vision Come From?

Where does vision come from? Is it innate? Does it come from a dream? Can it be taught? Most people think visioning is an internal process, something that just happens. Some people seem to be much better at this than others. However, as I learned from Dr. Bresler and his colleague Dr. Martin Rossman, people *can* learn visioning. All people can hone the ability to tap into their creative minds and enhance their creative skills. And in becoming more innovative, they can better lead their organizations to a more successful future.

Look around you at the room in which you are sitting. How did this room come into existence? Who imagined it? Who built it? Before the contractor or the builder began construction, someone had an idea to create a structure that included the room you are in. Before form came into existence, it was first an idea in someone's mind—a dream that became an envisioned reality.

To figure out how to tap into your imagination, you must first understand how the brain processes information. There are two information-processing systems in the central nervous system (CNS); one called *left-brain thinking*, which is linear or sequential, and another simultaneous (nonlinear) called *right-brain thinking*. You may already know that left-brain thinking is highly rational, logical, and analytical, and uses words in its thought processes. It is the "voice" of the conscious mind—that voice inside your head giving you guidance in words when you are awake.

Right-brain thinking, on the other hand, is sometimes called "lily-pad thinking" because thoughts are not interconnected in a linear fashion. The right brain is intuitive and can synthesize the big picture all at once. It uses images and symbols rather than words. It is also the language of the unconscious mind. When you dream, you don't dream in paragraphs or in words. Instead, you see pictures, which can help you better understand certain situations and help you solve problems that have stumped your rational, logical left brain.

Vision comes from an inner process that begins at birth and that we can access throughout our lives. We can consciously strengthen this process using visualization and imagery to stimulate our right brains, thereby developing our visioning ability.

While most people use both sides of the brain, they usually prefer one over the other. Some people have been highly trained in one way of thinking, and it is therefore especially hard for them to use the other side. Physicians, accountants, lawyers, and engineers, for example, are trained to use left-brain analytical thought predominantly, while artists, designers, and writers rely more on their right-brain creativity.

An example of extreme left-brain thinking is the process of "differential diagnosis," the system that physicians use to determine a diagnosis, beginning with the patient's presenting symptoms. Physicians use algorithmic steps—each of which consists of a test or series of tests—to make the final diagnosis. The test results then determine the following steps until all erroneous diagnoses have been ruled out.

On the other hand, many artists primarily use their right brains. They tap into their creative genius to produce paintings, sculpture, musical compositions, books, and other works of art. Unfortunately, problems can arise when right-brained artists fail to pay attention to their business affairs and finances—left-brain functions—and are taken advantage of by agents, managers, or professional money handlers. They could have avoided these situations if only they developed their left-brain function and paid closer attention to their business affairs.

# Creating an Organizational Vision

Imagination is crucial to developing a vision for your organization. It can also help you tackle difficult problems that stump your rational mind, because it allows you to find new approaches and workable solutions. Images help you access your inner wisdom and connect unrelated concepts in situations where reason and logic aren't cutting it.

Imagery can also help you suddenly experience an *aha* moment, a breakthrough. Albert Einstein is a good example of this phenomenon. He was not only a brilliant physicist at Princeton University, but he was also a great visualizer, famous for saying, "Imagination is more important than knowledge . . . knowledge is limited, but imagination encircles the world." He derived his $E=mc^2$ formula from his rational, brilliant left brain, combined with study of the earlier work of other scholars in the field, and also from imagining himself riding on the tip of a light beam holding a mirror in his hand and wondering if he could see his own reflection as he did so. This mental picture enabled him to bypass his rational mind and know that he had to square the speed of light in order to have the correct formula equating mass to energy.[2]

One extremely helpful visualization tool developed by Dr. Bresler and Dr. Rossman is called the Creative Inner Advisor.® This approach provides a way to connect with your inner wisdom by visualizing a kind, caring, loving, being who has only your best interest at heart. This being can be a person, living or dead, a fictitious character, an animal, or anything else you want to imagine.

To start, write down a question about your organization. Some examples might be:

What does the company's future look like?
In what direction should I lead?

How can I best motivate my workforce?

How can I solve a difficult problem?

Then use the guided imagery exercise that follows to ask your Creative Inner Advisor® to help you answer your question through imagery that contains new out-of-the-box ideas. You may find it helpful to read this exercise slowly into a tape recorder so that you can play it back and follow the instructions at a later time when you are certain you will not to be interrupted by your phone, your beeper, emails, friends, or family.

## Guided Imagery Exercise

I have used the following exercise to help participants recognize and develop a relationship with their Creative Inner Advisor.®

*Close your eyes, and sit comfortably in your chair. Focus your attention on your breathing. Feel yourself becoming more and more relaxed with each breath. Take a big breath in through your nose, and blow it out through your mouth. Take another big breath in through your nose, and blow it out through your mouth. Do this one more time.*

*Now imagine yourself in a very beautiful place. Take some time and look around you and fully appreciate your surroundings. Where are you? What time of day is it? What's the temperature? Do you hear any sounds? Experience all of the beauty of this place, the sights . . . the sounds . . . everything you feel here. [Pause]*

*As you look around, you see a being of some sort. It can be a person, an animal, or some other sort of creature; but it is kind, caring, and loving with only your best interest at heart. This being is your Creative Inner Advisor.® If you would like, you can give your Advisor a name and introduce yourself. [Pause]*

*Now ask your Inner Advisor the question concerning your organization about which you need guidance. Then listen quietly for the answer. [Pause] Note any images or sounds that come to mind. [Pause] Notice what you are feeling. [Pause] If you need to clarify anything your Inner Advisor says, please ask for that clarification and listen for the answer. [Pause]*

*Now it is time for you to take leave of your Creative Inner Advisor.® Finish your conversation, and ask your advisor to meet you again at a time in the future to go over how you are doing with your visioning or problem solving. Set a time to meet; then say good-bye. [Pause]*

*Focus your attention once again on your breathing. Breathe in through your nose . . . breathe out through your mouth . . . Breathe in through your nose . . . breathe out through your mouth . . . Breathe in through your nose . . . breathe out through your mouth. Slowly bring your attention back into the room you are in, and when you are ready, please open your eyes.*

You can use this exercise to create a new vision for your organization, or to imagine a personal vision for your life. It also may be quite helpful when you are trying to solve a Gordian-knot type of problem either in your company or in your life and are not sure where to start untying it. In situations like these, your logical left brain may not get you anywhere.

This exercise may produce an image from your inner resources that will help you come up with out-of-the-box solutions and strategies if you find yourself in a politically charged situation. You can make an appointment to talk things over with your Creative Inner Advisor® at any time. He or she may even just show up, perhaps in a dream, and help you solve your problem.

When I first began using this type of exercise at some of my leadership trainings, I was concerned that the professional world might think it was too far out there, and not recognize its power. I used this exercise as part of a leadership workshop for the Board of Trustees and the Board of Governors of the American College of Cardiology. I asked if anyone wanted to talk about the experience at the end, and no one raised a hand. I thought I had missed the mark completely—a surprise considering that my recent audience of physicians in California had been very talkative about their imagery experiences.

However, a number of cardiologists approached me after my presentation to tell me what they had visualized. A member of the Board of Trustees even came to the podium after the break and said, "What a great exercise that was! I polled a lot of you during the break and found advisors ranging from Jesus Christ to Jennifer Lopez."

I was very relieved to hear about how helpful this exercise had been for the cardiologists. Even though they were reluctant to let down their guard and talk about their experiences in a public setting, I know from follow-up calls that some were still getting advice from their Inner Advisors several years later. My coaching experience has shown what a valuable lifelong tool the Creative Inner Advisor® can become for current and would-be leaders everywhere. We all have inner wisdom; however, it takes effort to quiet our minds and remove ourselves from the day-to-day hustle and bustle to fully listen and understand what that wisdom has to offer us.

If perhaps your organization seems a little stagnant and you're worried that you might not be the most visionary leader, it can be helpful to listen to other people's ideas. Vision doesn't always have to come directly from you; it can come from a visionary on your board, or someone on your staff with a brilliant idea. Regardless of its source, it's imperative that you learn to recognize vision, accept it, and welcome it into the planning process.

Vision always comes from someone's internal resources. If you hear an idea that sounds terrific, always acknowledge and show appreciation for the person who shared it. It never hurts to give someone recognition by saying something like, "Jane has a wonderful idea that I think we should consider." As a leader, you may end up being responsible for implementing someone else's vision—and both you and your organization will ultimately benefit by doing so.

## Vision and Creative Problem Solving: Improving Patient Satisfaction in the Emergency Department

To demonstrate how the right brain and the left brain can work together to solve complex problems, let's look at a particularly difficult problem: improving patient satisfaction in a hospital's emergency department (ED). We can first use left-brain analytical methods by looking at Press Ganey patient satisfaction scores as described by Irwin Press in his book *Patient Satisfaction.*[3] As an emergency physician for 18 1/2 years, I concur with Press's assessment that the ED is a very special case; the patient is under a great deal of stress from pain, worry, and schedule disruption. Additionally, the emergency physician is under pressure and constantly multitasking. The one-time encounter in the ED between the patient and the doctor is supposed to make a positive impression so that the patient is satisfied with the visit and recommends the hospital to family and friends—a tall order, given the circumstances.

According to Press, an anthropologist, patient satisfaction can be increased through communication—even in this difficult situation. Patient satisfaction scores rose considerably and were not dependent on the total wait time if the patient was informed about what to expect at every step of the visit. Additionally, there were positive results when the amount of waiting time is overestimated on purpose, thereby setting an expectation that was met or exceeded.

Hospital employees can also use right-brain visualization to improve ED patient satisfaction. In some of my workshops, I use a guided imagery exercise in which I ask people to imagine that they are ED patients in their hospital, but no one knows who they are. They are then asked to visualize the entire visit, from onset of symptoms to arrival at the ED, registration, initial triage, assessment, tests, delivery of results, and disposition. By using visualization to experience what a patient endures, new ideas emerge that can improve patient satisfaction in addition to simply using the results of Press Ganey or other surveys. Using both left-brain and right-brain methods can produce the greatest results.

## Communicating and Creating Buy-In to Your Vision

If you have a great vision for your organization that you cannot communicate effectively, no one will follow it. And if you don't show passion for it, you will not gain support for it. Other people need to see your vision, feel your passion, and give you their all in helping to realize it.

Lack of passion isn't the only obstacle to effectively communicating a vision others follow. You'll limit your ability to persuade and motivate people to follow your lead if you do not connect with your audience and understand their needs.

If you find yourself in a predicament where you don't believe in your organization's vision—for example, if it's one that you inherited from your predecessors—you will either have to modify it so that you believe in it wholeheartedly and can communicate it enthusiastically, or create a new vision and lead your organization in a different direction about which you *do* feel passionately.

## Connecting with Your Audience

Leaders must know how to speak in front of an audience or a television camera. You have to connect with your audience no matter its size or the method of communication you use. If you are uncomfortable doing so, you will not be able to effectively communicate your vision or your passion.

There are many courses available that teach people how to be effective public speakers. Videotaping some of your presentations in advance is a great way to observe how you will appear in public and adjust your talk accordingly. Hiring a public-speaking coach to give you pointers may also be helpful, especially if you have to deliver a key speech. It can be invaluable to get direct feedback from a videotape and/or a coach.

Rapport is also essential to create buy-in to your vision. If you don't form a bond with your followers or are out of sync with them, they will probably not follow you—at least, not enthusiastically. They'll do it in order to keep their jobs. To form an effective connection with your followers, you need to listen to them in an effort to understand their wants and needs. Ask yourself: What motivates them? What do they care passionately about? What gets them excited?

It's helpful, when trying to build rapport with the people you want to support your vision, to remember Stephen Covey's fifth habit in *The 7 Habits of Highly Effective People*, which says, "Seek first to understand, then to be understood."[4] Bennis and Goldsmith echo this thought in their book *Learning to Lead* when they write that "Leaders must understand their followers, and followers must understand their leaders."[5] It is simply human nature to like people who understand us. Your followers are more likely to try to understand you and follow your vision if you have taken the time to understand them.

But what skills must a leader develop to gain this necessary understanding? In the following sections, I outline some important listening techniques and rapport-building tools that will help you better understand and motivate others. These tools will help you build trust, create highly effective teams of people, and motivate others to follow your vision.

## Listening

Listening is a skill that most of us could practice more often. This point became clear to me soon after I became a headhunter. My experience as an emergency physician made it very hard for me to initially figure out what headhunting was all about. So I paid a visit to a senior partner at Heidrick & Struggles who had been an executive at a major pharmaceutical company. He was used to working with doctors, and I thought he could give me a few pointers. I told him I didn't really understand what I was supposed to be doing, and he politely said, "Shut up and listen." It turned out to be the best piece of advice I could have received at the time; I paid more attention to my clients' needs and was able to conduct better organizational assessments and make better placements as a result.

I also learned at Heidrick that all people like to talk about themselves. I started encouraging my clients to talk, which was surprisingly easy to do. People truly love it when others listen to them; it compels them to think that you care about them.

Two tips for improving your listening skills are "listening with presence" and "active listening." **Listening with presence** involves quieting your mind and focusing completely on the other person. Your body language should reflect this focus; you want to make eye contact, lean forward, or even take a few notes. Your attention is in the present moment, and you aren't judging them. You don't let your mind wander, not even to contemplate what you need to do before your next meeting or think about how bored you are in your present situation. When listening with presence you must be totally focused and listening to the words of the person before you. People will react very favorably when you, as a listener, are totally focused on them.

**Active listening** means that you repeat back a snippet of what you just heard. For example, I interviewed a candidate for an academic position at a large university medical center who described his research in great detail. I repeated back a short recap partway through his lengthy description: "So you have an RO1 grant from the NIH for $1 million studying liver metabolism over the next two years that is portable to your new institution." This short synopsis confirmed what the candidate had said, and let him know that I had heard and understood him. People like to know that someone is paying attention to them and hears what they are saying. Therefore, this is a critical leadership skill to master.

Fully listening and understanding another person involves more than just what we hear, though. What we see and feel—our "sixth sense" or intuition—are also involved. A classic communications study from the University of Pennsylvania revealed that the spoken word represents only about 7 percent of what is communicated in an interchange between two people. Tone of voice accounts for approximately 38 percent, and nonverbal communication is approximately 55 percent.[6] See Figure 6.1.

It's best to communicate in person to fully appreciate everything that is expressed during a conversation. An in-person meeting allows you to observe all of the nonverbal cues that are present.

While almost everyone uses email these days, we must remember that electronic messages do not include either tone of voice or

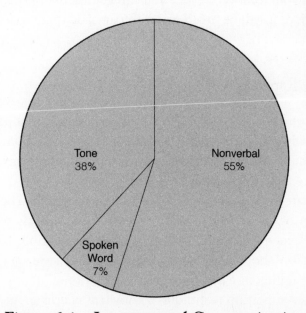

**Figure 6.1 Interpersonal Communication**

nonverbal communication. You can add an exclamation mark, smiley face, or frown; but none of these make up for the complete lack of in-person interaction. According to the statistic cited earlier, e-mail only accounts for about 7 percent of what a person may be trying to express—leaving 93 percent unsaid. This is why many emails—especially in terms of tone—are misinterpreted, thereby causing unnecessary difficulties among co-workers.

While voicemail is better than email, it's not perfect. Since it allows you to express both tone of voice and spoken words, you deliver approximately 45 percent of your intended communication. However, you will still miss certain nuances of body language—a clenched fist, crossed arms, and so forth—that you would have seen if you had communicated in-person. I always recommend conducting important negotiations or interviews face-to-face so that both parties can see and interpret nonverbal communication.

If you want to build rapport and gain support for your vision, try listening with *all* of your senses instead of selling your great ideas by talking *at* your followers. Once you can get a sense of their position and opinion, it will be much easier to persuade them to follow your lead.

## Building Rapport

It is important to remember when building rapport that people like working with people who are—or seem to be—like them. Having to interact with someone who seems very different may result in reluctance to follow.

There are some easy first steps in building rapport. Though they may seem obvious, they're vital in connecting quickly with other people. Remember to start with a friendly greeting, focus your attention on the other person, express enthusiasm, and give an honest compliment early on in your interaction.

Another important technique is known as *matching and mirroring*, in which you subtly match and mirror something about another person's body language and/or nonverbal communication. It is based on the premise cited earlier: that most people want to do business with their friends or people like them. You can use nonverbal means to reflect similarity to establish rapport quickly.

One way to match and mirror somebody with your body language is to sit with your legs crossed, for example, if the other person is doing the same. If a person has his or her hand on the table between you, you can also have your hand on the table. You may also want to match the speed at which your colleague speaks. If they're talking very quickly, you can talk very quickly. If you talk slowly, you will seem dissimilar to them, instead of seeming like a familiar match. You can also use your attire, posture, facial expressions, gestures, eye contact, touch, or proximity.

Keep in mind, however, that it is critical to do all this subtly. Only try to match and mirror one or two things at a time; if you try to do everything all a once, you will come across as an obvious carbon copy and appear comical. It's a good idea to practice this outside of the workplace until you become proficient at it. The following story proves this point.

I had to meet with eight partners in one day when I first interviewed with Heidrick & Struggles for a consultant position. By the fifth or sixth interview, I began thinking that each partner was mirroring me. It was a very odd feeling; in fact, a bit creepy! I knew by the seventh interview that the interviewer was not a decision maker about my hiring, so I decided to test my hypothesis. I crossed my legs, and the partner crossed his. I deliberately crossed my legs in the other direction, and he quickly followed suit . . . not too subtle. I then started to cross my legs in the opposite direction, but stopped in mid stream, returning to my original crossed leg position. The partner, who was mirroring me, got his legs caught halfway in the middle, not knowing which way to finish crossing them. I knew for sure that I was being mirrored and decided that the interviewers must have been taught this technique somewhere.

After joining the firm, sure enough, I learned at New Consultant Orientation how to match and mirror as a way to establish rapport with our clients. The preceding story shows why it's crucial to be understated when using matching and mirroring. You need to establish familiarity at an almost subconscious level.

## Neuro-Linguistic Programming (NLP)

Headhunters also use a technique known as neuro-linguistic programming (NLP) to build rapport with their clients. NLP is a special form of matching and mirroring developed in the 1970s at the University of California at Santa Cruz by linguistic professor John Grinder and psychology student Richard Bandler. Although some of their findings have been contested in the literature, NLP has remained a helpful rapport-building tool in many situations.

Grinder and Bandler determined that people use different senses in what they defined to be primary modes of communication. Some people are visual communicators, some are auditory, and some are kinesthetic (those who communicate best through touch or feeling).

NLP states that everyone has a favored mode of communication when they're young—visual, auditory, or kinesthetic. We prefer to learn and also express ourselves through this same mode. However, we learn to use all three modes at various times as we get older. One way to establish rapport with someone quickly is to determine their primary mode of communication and mirror it back. By doing so, you will effectively be speaking the same language and reflect similarity.

I first learned NLP from an emergency physician who taught communication skills at Stanford University. During crises—which happen daily in emergency departments—people revert to their preferred mode of communication. Emergency physicians have very little time to build rapport with patients. They must get in sync with them almost immediately and encourage patients to trust them and tell them what is wrong in a very limited period of time. Emergency physicians also want to establish rapport so that patients are more likely to follow their aftercare instructions. NLP can help accomplish all of these things.

My sister, Kathie Rovetti, an elementary school music teacher for 37 years, used NLP in her classroom. Since her young students all had a preference about which of their primary senses they used, my sister taught using visual, auditory, and kinesthetic methods. She had pictures of composers and colored notes on the walls of her classroom for the visual learners; she played music tapes, CDs, and instruments for the auditory learners; and she had drums, autoharps, and other instruments for the kinesthetic (tactile) learners to touch and play.

Many actors, TV reporters, and politicians have also learned to use NLP to connect with their audiences effectively. Well-known personal performance guru Tony Robbins has been able to use NLP to predict the outcome of presidential elections in the United States based on how well each candidate was able to use all three modes of communication, as well as whether their actions seemed to match their words. According to Robbins, the best leaders can use all three modes to connect with their followers, who then are more likely to believe in the candidates' personal integrity.

To test Robbins's assertion, we can review the 2008 presidential and vice-presidential elections in the United States. Two candidates—Barack Obama and Sarah Palin—were not well known by many Americans, but both used the three elements of NLP quite effectively to further their candidacies. They looked good in front of a crowd and on TV (Palin even dressed herself and her family in Armani for maximal visual effect); they sounded good when delivering scripted speeches; and their words evoked feelings from the crowd. As a communications major at the University of Idaho who then became a TV broadcaster, Palin was no doubt aware of NLP. It helped her, but only to a point: her interview with Katie Couric contained some unscripted responses that sounded like gibberish. Additionally, her confused, deer-in-the-headlights appearance didn't reassure visual viewers, and her incomprehensible words were especially unpleasant to auditory communicators.

Palin simply did not seem credible as a serious vice presidential candidate.

On the other hand, Obama looked good, sounded good, and could elicit strong feelings from the crowds he addressed throughout the campaign. He did the same during his unscripted interviews. Hillary Rodham Clinton looked and sounded good, but seemed cold and emotionless in front of audiences. Her kinesthetic mode proved to be her weakness—except when her voice cracked the night before the election in the New Hampshire primary, revealing true emotion. In fact, she likely won that primary in part because she showed her kinesthetic side to voters. John McCain did not look as energetic and vital as Obama or Palin. He sounded pretty good except when his anger was evident. Although he typically did not stir crowds to great heights of enthusiasm, as did Obama, the story of his experience as a prisoner of war at the Hanoi Hilton in Vietnam would elicit feeling from anyone. Overall, Obama was the most effective user of NLP—a skill that helped a little-known U.S. senator from Illinois become President of the United States.

## Are You Visual, Auditory, or Kinesthetic?

It is important to be able to use all three modes of communication as a leader, and to adapt your preferred mode to your audience. But how do you know what someone's preferred mode is? It can be a bit complicated and takes practice to figure it out, but there are ways to do so. You can look at people's attire, consider their occupation, and listen to their speech patterns as well as the words they use.

Visual communicators care about the way things look. They dress very well, and usually have beautifully decorated homes. They work in visual professions such as painting, designing, architecture, or photography. They tend to speak in an energized, rapid manner, and use words that have a visual connotation such as:

"That **looks** like a good idea."

"I **see** what you mean."

"I get the **picture**."

"Let me **shed some light** on the subject."

Auditory communicators like the way things sound. They enjoy listening to music, books on tape, and talking on the telephone. Their typical occupations include musician, sound engineer, telephone salesperson, and lawyer. (Remember, lawyers even bill for their phone time.) They tend to speak in a melodic, easy-to-listen-to fashion and use words that have an auditory connotation like:

"I **hear** what you're saying."

"That **sounds** great to me."

"**Tell** me what you think."

"That **rings a bell** with me."

People who are kinesthetic communicators relate to others through touch or feeling. They like activities that make them feel good such as running, dancing, and working out—activities that get their endorphins flowing. They also may like lying in the sun, or eating and drinking; again, because these things make them feel good. They prefer to dress in comfortable clothes and have homes with comfortable furniture. Their speech pattern tends to be slow and drawn out, with sighs and pauses as they experience the feelings they are discussing. Their words emote a feeling or a sense of touch such as:

"What do you **feel** like doing?"

"I **understand** how you feel."

"Let's keep in **touch**."

"I'm very **shook up** over his leaving."

Remembering all of these things take practice. However, learning NLP is worth the investment of time since it has proven to be a valuable rapport-building tool that will help you connect with and motivate your audiences large and small.

## NLP Mismatch

In working with physicians on management teams, I have observed a significant NPL mismatch problem. In the general population, over 80 percent of people are visual communicators, about 10 percent are auditory, and only 5 to 7 percent are kinesthetic.[7] However, from my own testing, over 50 percent of physicians are primarily kinesthetic communicators, which puts us in a small minority when compared to the American norm. Physicians relate through touch and use feeling words; we are in a very physical profession that requires us to lay our hands, literally, on patients. We palpate, we percuss, and we even operate inside our patients' bodies—not something most people do on a day-to-day basis.

As kinesthetic communicators, physicians tend to speak slowly as they express their feelings. Excluding plastic surgeons, who, based on my own research, are predominantly visual, physicians are not known to be the best dressers; they may in fact prefer the comfort of scrubs or their white coat, even in management meetings.

Many corporate CEOs are visual communicators, as are most marketing people. They love charts, graphs, and PowerPoint presentations and tend to speak quickly. Imagine a meeting between a hospital CEO and a physician executive, such as the Senior Vice President of Medical Affairs. The CEO is well-dressed, talks fast and intensely, and sees the big picture. The doctor talks slowly, sighs often, is wearing scrubs and a white coat, has no PowerPoint presentation, and says, "I really feel we should proceed with this disease state management program." Although both are speaking English, they are not communicating their thoughts and ideas as effectively as possible because they are using different communication modes to express themselves.

The good news is that you can learn to shift your communication mode depending on your audience. Learning to use visual, auditory, and kinesthetic modes of communication proficiently will help you build rapport quickly and communicate better with your followers.

And it will be much easier to create buy-in to your vision once you've established rapport—thereby leading your organization to new levels of success and prosperity.

## Leading with Vision: The Story of Meriter Medical Group

The story of Madison, Wisconsin–based Meriter Medical Group (MMG) provides an excellent example of how an organization can create and share a compelling vision. MMG is an employed physician group wholly owned by Meriter. Based on a scan of their local healthcare marketplace, which was dominated by the University of Wisconsin and the Dean Clinic, Meriter developed a vision and strategy to create its own clinically integrated delivery system.

Part of their overarching vision was to build an employed physician group starting in 2007 with just 12 hospital-based physicians. MMG now has nearly 100 physicians at multiple sites and has invested heavily in infrastructure to support the physician practices. It is rated number one in patient satisfaction in Madison, and is more closely aligned with Physicians Plus Insurance Corporation (P-Plus, for short), a regional insurance carrier. MMG's vision statement reads as follows:

> *Simply to "Be the Best"* . . .
> * The Best Place for Patients to Receive Care
> * The Best Place for Physicians to Practice
> * The Best Place for Staff to Work

The group's envisioned future includes being a multispecialty group of over 200 physicians and serving as the primary provider for P-Plus insurance, providing over 95 percent of P-Plus patients' healthcare needs, and being a market leader in clinical quality, patient satisfaction, and cost.

In his book entitled *Leading Change*, leadership guru John Kotter emphasizes how important it is to use every vehicle possible to communicate a change vision.[8] In my opinion, MMG has done just that. Working with President Dr. Robert Turngren and Meriter Chief Medical Officer Dr. Geoffrey Priest, I developed a yearlong physician leadership program for MMG's Leadership Council and Service Line Directors. Both Dr. Turngren and Dr. Priest presented the MMG vision at each of these meetings. Clinic managers were included in the meetings so that they could pass the vision on to the nonphysician staff. Dr. Turngren presented the vision again at the MMG Annual Meeting, which was attended by about 200 physicians and staff members. The group has a sense of accomplishment and forward momentum to date, but needs to do more work to make the envisioned future a reality. However, MMG's leaders' ability to communicate their compelling vision effectively provides the impetus to move forward.

In the next chapter, I will outline a strategic planning process that will help you create an action plan for making your vision for organizational success a reality. But first what follows is your next prescription for success that recaps the key points in this chapter.

## The Prescription: Planning Part 1 – Creating and Communicating a Vision

1. Conduct an environmental scan so that you fully understand marketplace trends and can better anticipate your customers' needs.

2. Using the guided imagery exercise in this chapter, create a vision for your organization that incorporates the information you discovered during the environmental scan.

3. You may also want to use the same exercise to create a vision for your life and career.

4. Use your imagination and visioning to develop new strategies and solutions to any difficult problems.

5. Communicate your organizational vision throughout your company using every means possible.

6. Establish rapport with your audiences and make an effort to listen and better understand their needs before trying to persuade them to follow you.

7. If necessary, seek help from a professional speech coach using videotaping to provide feedback before speaking in front of an audience.

CHAPTER

# 7

# Developing a Strategic Plan for Organizational Transformation

*Begin with the end in mind.*
—Stephen R. Covey, *The 7 Habits of Highly Effective People,*
"Habit 2"

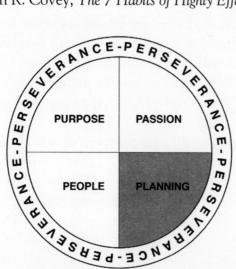

T he next step in your organization's transformation process is to develop a strategic plan that includes goals and objectives that will move your organization from where it is today to where you ideally want to be. Although you have aligned your organization's purpose with the marketplace, ignited passion in your company, and created a compelling vision that implies forward movement, your organization will not reach its goals and maximize its success without a realistic plan of action. You must combine vision with action if it is to become more than just a dream.

## Internal and External Organizational Analysis

At the start of any planning process it is essential to have an understanding of trends in your marketplace. The information that you obtain from a market analysis or environmental scan will serve as a strong foundation for developing strategic goals and objectives.

I always have retreat attendees complete a SWOT analysis—for strengths, weaknesses, opportunities, and threats—prior to facilitating any strategic planning. I want to know in advance what they perceive to be the organization's internal strengths and weaknesses, as well as the external opportunities and threats. The responses make it fairly clear what issues the organization is grappling with and in what areas they need to set goals to move forward. Sometimes organizational leaders are aware of how the company functions internally, but many need to receive more up-to-date information about external or marketplace forces that can either propel or hinder their success.

I usually give my healthcare clients an update about late-breaking news in the healthcare industry. Many changes have occurred recently due to the implementation of the Affordable Care Act, the move towards electronic medical records, and the arrival of payment reform. I also discuss local market issues. No matter what the industry, it is a good idea to get the lay of the land—specifically, to have a discussion or presentation on external marketplace trends—before working on goals and objectives.

# Goal Setting

Knowing where you want your company to go is critical to its success. As the great Yankees catcher Yogi Berra is quoted as saying, *"If you don't know where you are going, you will wind up somewhere else."* Setting goals for your organization is essential for growth and prosperity, which is why there are many goal-setting processes in the literature, often accompanied by an identifying acronym. One of my favorites is the SMART Goals method.[1] Madison, Wisconsin–based Meriter Medical Group (MMG)—whose successes we mentioned in the previous chapter—uses this approach. The SMART acronym stands for the following:

S = Specific and Strategic
M = Measurable
A = Attainable
R = Relevant/Rigorous
T = Time Bound

Each letter represents a key ingredient that is required for a strategic plan to succeed. First, the goal must be **specific**. What are people supposed to do? By when? Who is doing it? At what cost? It must be **strategic** in that it places the organization in the best position for success. If the goal is for a subsidiary, then it must also be part of the parent company's overarching strategic plan.

Organizations must be able to **measure** each goal so that they stay on target. Without measurement, it is too easy to slip off track and fail to reach goals in a timely fashion—or at all. The goal must also be **attainable**. To ensure this, it is important to measure each step along the way. Doing so allows you to provide feedback to your team about any progress being made, and assure them that they can attain the ultimate goal. Companies need to ask questions like: Is there enough time, money, talent, and resources to accomplish the goal? If you can't accomplish the goal because one of these items is lacking, then it is not worth pursuing.

The goal must be **relevant** to the organization's core purpose and values. If it isn't, it will be hard to motivate your workforce to take action to achieve it. People need to see value in their efforts, and not consider their hard work a waste of time. A goal should also be **rigorous,** in that it challenges employees to give their best effort but not *so* rigorous that they are doomed to fail.

Being **time bound** means that you hold the goal to a timeline for success. I prefer two- or three-year strategic plans with measurable checkpoints along the way, because I find that they're more realistic and attainable. Five-year plans are all too frequently filed away on a shelf until $4^1/_2$ years have gone by, at which point they are dusted off to see, if by any chance, the organization has hit its goals. One client of mine had a *40-year* strategic plan, with the noble goal of ending poverty in the region during that time frame. Although such a goal can be inspiring, it is not practical on a day-to-day basis. It is better to break such a high reaching goal down into doable two- or three-year increments that are measurable and attainable.

I cannot overstate how crucial it is to set goals. Harvard University researchers conducted a study (often quoted in business literature) that found that only *3 percent* of Harvard students set goals for themselves. This surprising fact was even more significant some 30 years later, when they discovered in a follow-up study that these same 3 percent were the most successful and held 50 percent of the total net worth of the entire group of students.[2]

Setting goals helps establish intention, and forces people to expend their energy, time, and resources in the direction of the goal. Similarly, writing these goals down makes your entire organization aware of your commitment to achieving them. Clear goals become the action plan that will help make your vision a reality.

## The Working-Backwards Process

The vision you have developed for your organization should be an inspiring one that motivates your employees to give their best effort. However, you need to divide most visions into workable steps that everyone involved can accomplish within the time frame you establish.

As cited at the beginning of this chapter, Habit 2 in Stephen Covey's acclaimed *The 7 Habits of Highly Effective People* is "Begin with the end in mind."[3] Working backwards from your vision helps to assure that you will actually reach it. If you start by moving forward from your current situation, your goals may not be far-sighted enough. You risk falling short of the mark because you're focusing on short-terms goals and objectives rather than on the big picture—thereby limiting your success.

## Developing Three to Five Specific Organizational Goals

Companies frequently use strategic-planning retreats to determine and prioritize specific organizational goals and objectives. Although the words "goals" and "objectives" can be used interchangeably according to Webster's dictionary, I use the word "goals" at such retreats to mean the major endpoints that will lead to making the corporate vision a reality. I use "objectives" to refer to lesser targets under each goal that will lead to the successful attainment of that goal.

You can determine goals and identify key issues for retreat attendees to work on by using the results of the SWOT analysis done prior to a retreat. In order to keep the planning session focused, I pick only the top three to five issues to address instead of everything mentioned beforehand. I divide the retreat attendees into groups that address each of these key issues based on interest (passion), knowledge, and experience, and even allow people to participate in more than one group if time permits. I have each group brainstorm about strategies to deal with their issue, then ask them to develop one or two goals to propose to the entire group that will address the issue and move the company forward toward its vision.

Before proposing a goal, each breakout group should test it against the SMART Goals criteria to make sure it is workable, and also against the organization's core values. Any goal that conflicts with a core value should be altered in order to maintain organizational integrity.

## Developing Two to Four Specific Objectives for Each Goal

Each breakout group must also propose two to four objectives for each goal they recommend. It's best to limit the number of objectives to two to four per goal in order to maintain focus, since too many objectives can cause confusion and impede progress. Again, you want to test each objective against your company's core values and eliminate any that conflict.

Next, each breakout group proposes their goals and its objectives to all retreat participants. The entire group will then look critically at three things—time, talent, and treasure—to make sure the goals and objectives are realistic and doable.

## Time: Create a Timeline for Each Step

After the groups have proposed their goals and objectives, everyone needs to work together to develop a timeline for achieving each step. Work backwards from your vision to figure out what sequence of goals you should follow to achieve your vision. When do you want to reach each goal? With those target dates in mind, when will you need to accomplish each objective along the way?

You might also want to diagram a flow chart to help everyone understand the goal-setting process. Begin by putting your vision in a box near the top-right corner of a blank piece of flip chart paper, and then place your current situation in a box near the bottom-left corner of the same flip chart paper, as shown in Figure 7.1.

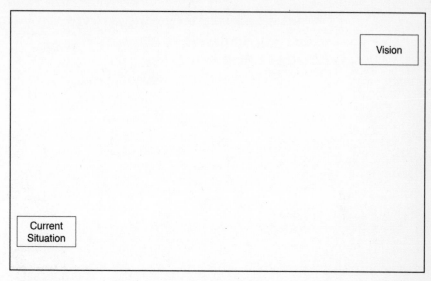

**Figure 7.1  Your Vision versus Your Current Situation**

Figure 7.2 shows the process of putting your goals in place by working backwards from the organizational vision.

You'll then want to diagram the time frame for all of your goals on the flow chart. You should place items that have target dates in

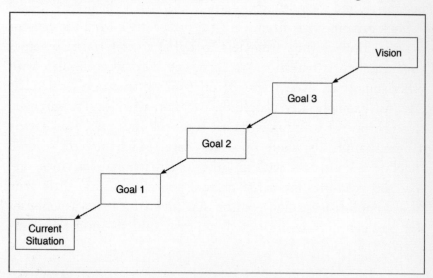

**Figure 7.2  Working Backwards to Set Goals**

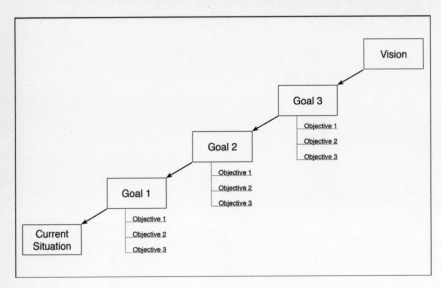

**Figure 7.3    Adding Objectives**

the near future on the left side of the chart, closest to your current situation. Write in the objectives under each goal, as shown in Figure 7.3, and include target dates next to each objective.

Look at your chart from a critical perspective, from the present moving forward (i.e., from left to right) to determine whether your timeline is realistic. Are there any dates that conflict with other important events already on your organization's calendar? Are, for example, key people on vacation when you're supposed to reach one of your target dates? Is one of your presenters giving a presentation elsewhere on a key date? Make sure the overall timeline is consistent with all other organizational activities, and that the deadlines are achievable. If you allocate too little time to accomplish a specific goal or objective, the team assigned to the goal can become frustrated and demoralized—and will likely produce suboptimal results at best, and disappointing, or no results at worst.

One real-life example of this working-backwards process took place a decade ago when I had a vision to create a physician leadership institute. I was an executive search consultant at the time, and occasionally gave presentations on physician leadership. I had also helped sponsor the study on physician executive success factors that MBA students at UCLA's Anderson School of Management had conducted, mentioned in the previous chapter.

In order to reach my vision, I created four goals as follows:

1. Develop a curriculum.
2. Develop a nationally known faculty.
3. Develop a marketing plan.
4. Build infrastructure.

I knew after reviewing my timeline I had to establish the curriculum *before* I recruited the faculty. I also knew that because you never market a bad product, we'd need to establish the curriculum, faculty, and infrastructure before launching a large-scale marketing plan. The working-backwards diagram for these four goals would look like Figure 7.4.

Each goal included its own objectives. For example, I needed to review the market analysis I had done for the American Medical Association (AMA) about physician career needs and also do a literature review in order to create the curriculum. Another objective for that goal was to conduct interviews with key people, including past and present physician leaders, CEOs who work with physicians, and support staff who deal with physicians on a regular basis. Each of my four goals had two to four objectives that I prioritized according to time.

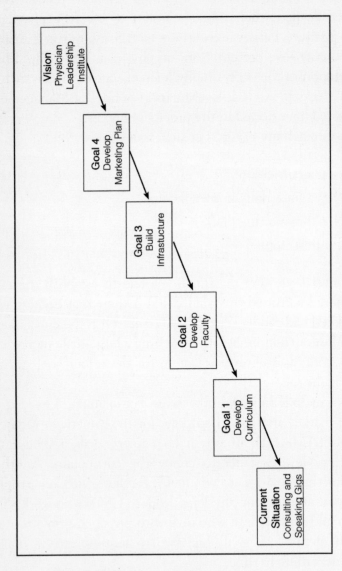

Figure 7.4   A Sample Working-Backwards Diagram

## Talent: Build Your Team

The next step in developing your plan is to have the group consider what type of people they'll need to accomplish each goal and objective, and write that on the chart. This process will help you begin to build the team that executes the strategic plan. As a leader, you have no doubt assembled teams of competent people who have executed action plans in the past. You therefore know that a key element of strategic planning is assigning the responsibility of accomplishing a certain goal and/or objective to the *right* person—or the *right* team of people. The process may fall short if you select someone who doesn't quite fit—simply because he or she wasn't up to the task. You must build a team of people who share your vision and can help you reach your goals on time and with the resources available by following through on the tasks they receive.

As Jim Collins says in *Good to Great*, it is very important to "have the right people on the bus."[4] In fact, he urges leaders to do this even *before* you work on your vision or your strategy, and I agree. It is best to create a corporate vision and strategy with the right people present from the beginning. It is also critical to decide which people will execute the strategy once the leaders have pointed the way.

## Treasure: Determine What Resources You Need

The strategic planning group must also consider what resources they'll need to accomplish each goal and objective, and then add these to the flow chart. Some resources to consider include money, equipment, supplies, support staff, training, and any others you may think of as you review your flow chart or talk with your team. Try to make the list as comprehensive as possible. If you leave something off the list, you may overestimate whether the goal is doable. One specific resource may be crucial for reaching your goal, and its omission will cause failure that you could have prevented.

## Do a Reality Check

Before the participants at a strategic planning meeting prioritize the proposed goals and objectives, I ask the managers, who will be responsible for executing the plan, to give the leadership group who created the plan a reality check. Is the plan doable? Do they have enough time to get everything done? Is there enough staff to support the plan? Are there enough resources available to execute the plan in a timely manner? This reality check will help determine whether the plan's goals and objectives are too overreaching—and if it might lead to frustration and disappointment rather than optimal success.

## Prioritizing Goals and Objectives

No organization can do all things or be all things to all people. It is therefore very important to prioritize the goals and objectives based on the following factors:

1. Do they *advance the organization* toward its vision?
2. Are they *doable in the time frame* allotted?
3. Is there *enough talent available* to execute the plan?
4. Are there *enough resources available* during the allotted time period to support the activities?

Retreat participants consider these questions and then vote, usually by putting color-coded or numbered Post-its next to each goal. As the facilitator, I tally the votes to determine which goals will be the organization's primary focus. I then plot the top-priority goals and objectives on a doable timeline, creating a final flow chart. This chart will also list which team members will be held accountable and the resources needed next to each goal and objective.

## Remain Open to New Opportunities

It is important to avoid fixating on your ultimate outcome when finalizing your goals and objectives. Becoming overly attached to a particular element of the plan may cause you to shut yourself off from future opportunities that present themselves as the marketplace changes—opportunities that may be far superior to what you had originally envisioned. New possibilities and avenues will likely pass you by unless you remain open to exploring them when they appear.

In the mid-1990s the Malibu disasters forced me to do some goal setting of my own in order to honor my financial commitments, which seemed quite overwhelming at the time. So I decided to try a goal-setting process I read about in *The Seven Spiritual Laws of Success* by Dr. Deepak Chopra.[5] Chopra suggests that you write down your goals (or your intention) and put them in a place where you can see them frequently. Then he describes a meditative process in which you release your goals into the gap between thoughts, into what he calls "the field of pure potentiality." By doing so, you free yourself from becoming too attached to a particular outcome.

The goal I wrote down was to get a job based in Los Angeles, at which I would make enough money to pay off all of my debts. The date I set to achieve this was Christmas 1995. I got more specific by adding the dollar amount I wanted to earn, and it was more money than I had ever dreamed of making. I also added a signing bonus to my written goal. I kept my goal somewhere visible day and night, and meditated every morning and night, doing my best to follow Dr. Chopra's process.

When I first set my goal, I thought I would be joining Russell Reynolds, the executive search firm that had first approached me about becoming a search professional. But the more I mediated on my goals, the more I realized that I was not attached to *that* particular outcome. So when another leading international search firm, Heidrick & Struggles, got in touch with me, I found myself pleased at the prospect of being pursued by both firms. It seems that setting my goal twice a day had made me quite popular. Not only did two major international search firms want me to work for them, but renowned professional services firm Ernst & Young *and* two healthcare companies did as well. All were very worthwhile positions to consider, but in the end, I knew what I wanted to do. I received an offer from Heidrick for a job based in Los Angeles right around Christmas of 1995—an offer for which I would be paid the *exact* salary amount and signing bonus that I had written down in my goals. Because I wasn't overly attached to the original anticipated outcome, I was able to seize a greater opportunity that came my way.

## Telling Others about Your Goals—A Word of Caution

It is wise—in fact, essential—to share your goals with other member members of your organization. It is clear from your flow chart that every step requires people to work as a team to reach these goals. Everyone needs to understand the vision and the goals that have been set before them. There is also great benefit from brainstorming with others, as opposed to operating in silos on specific, individual tasks. Synergy often happens when two or more groups meet to solve a problem or develop a strategy together.

A word of caution, however: You need trustworthy people to execute your plan, and you must make sure that they don't leak trade secrets to your competition. If they are inspired by the corporate vision, in sync with the company's core values, and trust the organization's leadership, they are most likely to be trustworthy in return.

# Create a Feedback Loop to Assess Your Progress on a Quarterly Basis, and Adjust Your Plan Accordingly

I once read that a plane flying from Los Angeles to New York City does not fly in a straight line – as many people might assume it does. Instead, the pilots or autopilots on these flights constantly monitor their flight path, adjusting the course according to the feedback they receive from the plane's monitoring equipment. In much the same way, you must check in with your team at regular intervals to see what progress you're making. Skipping this important step will most likely cause you to drift off course, and hinder your progress toward your goal. You'll never achieve an action plan in its entirety unless you engage in a regular, ongoing assessment of your progress, which will allow you to adjust your plan as needed. Is your team ahead of schedule or is it falling behind? If so, why? Do you need to alter future dates and targets? Holding regular brainstorming sessions with your team is an excellent way to stay on track and take the best path to optimal success.

# Reward Your Team for Reaching Milestones

Rewarding good behavior is a very important conditioning tool. We humans respond to positive reinforcement, so in addition to the dates, people, and resources listed on your flow chart, make sure you also write down rewards you'll give for achieving important accomplishments along the way. These rewards should be significant to you and your team, things that are fun and motivating, and that express your appreciation for a job well done.

To make sure your rewards are appropriate and delivered in a timely way, create a list in advance of several things that you consider to be excellent rewards. I've listed some reward ideas my clients have had success with in the past. Of course, the reward you choose must fit within your budget, so my list of suggestions includes different price ranges. I've left some spaces for you to write down your own ideas. You will then have a ready list to consult whenever you reach a milestone and will have no excuse for procrastination.

---

### Rewards

1. Surprise lunch for the team on-site (e.g., order in pizza or Chinese food) _____

2. Off-site celebration (e.g., cocktail party, dinner with entertainment)_____

3. Company picnic with family activities _____

4. Sporting event (e.g., Lakers game, a day at the races, Super Bowl party)

5. Starbucks cards or other gift certificates _____

6. _____

7. _____

8. _____

9. _____

10. _____

---

The strategic planning process outlined in this chapter will create a road map for your organization that will help make your compelling vision a reality. Remember to be patient and persistent as you work through this process. The 5th P, which we will discuss in detail in Chapter 9, is Perseverance, without which lasting success may not be possible.

## Personal Strategic Planning

Strategic planning is essential for leaders to be highly effective within their organizations. And while most leaders have led or participated in strategic planning processes for their companies, surprisingly few have ever created such a plan for themselves. When I ask CEOs in my audiences how many have a strategic plan for their own lives, very few raise their hands.

One of my executive coaching clients, a strategic planner for hospitals and health systems, was amazed when I asked her this question. Although she had worked on many strategic plans in her job, it simply never occurred to her to create a plan for her life. It suddenly dawned on her that her life was not moving forward because she had no personal plan of action.

Because leaders need to be clear about their own personal goals as they move their organizations forward, you can use the same process described earlier to develop a strategic plan for your life.

The next chapter will cover ways to develop people and build effective teams within your organization. This will help your corporate vision, goals, and objectives become reality. But first, here is your prescription for success that recaps the key points in this chapter.

# The Prescription: Planning Part 2—Developing a Strategic Plan

1. Do a thorough market analysis or environmental scan to help you understand trends in your marketplace.

2. Invite key organizational leaders to participate in a strategic planning meeting. Ask each invitee to complete a SWOT analysis—an evaluation of the organization's internal Strengths and Weaknesses and its external Opportunities and Threats—prior to the meeting.

3. Form break-out groups at the meeting, and ask each to develop four or five goals for each issue the SWOT analysis identified. Then have the groups develop two to four objectives for each goal. Make sure that the goals and objectives do not conflict with your organization's core values, and eliminate any that do.

4. Create a timeline for each goal and objective. Work backwards from the corporate vision, and place the goals and objectives on a flow chart that diagrams the steps needed to achieve the vision.

5. Assign people to be held accountable for reaching each goal or objective in a timely manner.

6. Assure that you have adequate resources, people and time to accomplish each goal and objective by doing a reality check with the management team.

7. Prioritize the goals and objectives based on steps 4 to 7 above.

8. Communicate your goals and objectives throughout the organization to maximize synergy.

9. Set up a feedback loop to assess progress made each quarter on reaching goals and objectives. Reward your team for reaching milestones!

10. Remain open to new opportunities that present themselves along the way.

11. As a leader, use the same process to create a personal strategic plan for your life and career.

CHAPTER

8

# Developing People, Transforming Your Culture

*Teamwork is the ability to work together toward a common vision, the ability to direct individual accomplishment toward organizational objectives. It is the fuel that allows common people to attain uncommon results.*

—Anonymous

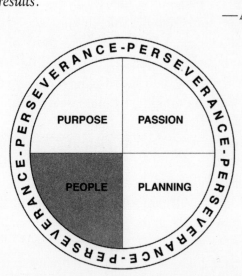

123

Zappos CEO Tony Hsieh, whom I first mentioned in Chapter 4, quoted his company's philosophy in his *20/20* interview with Barbara Walters:

*Great things will happen if you make employees happy.*

Hsieh went on to explain,

*We want to celebrate each person's individuality.*[1]

The company's core values clearly reflect a focus on not only excellent service, but also on developing people—an element that is crucial to the company's great success.

## The Value of the Right Human Capital

It was not until I got to the recruiting firm Heidrick & Struggles that I learned to fully appreciate the value of human capital—not just *any* human capital, but the right human capital. I knew as the CEO of an emergency medical center that at least half of my expenses were payroll expenses. And when I became a consultant in the healthcare industry, I saw that most of my clients were also spending at least 50 percent on salaries for their employees as well.

I was initially surprised by the amount we charged for our search fees at Heidrick, which were one-third of the successful candidate's total cash compensation (including base salary and bonuses). But then I saw data showing how placing the right CEO at an organization can dramatically increase its value. You can't just appoint any CEO. It has to be the right one.

A recent study on succession planning by James Citrin and Dayton Ogden, consultants at leading international search firm Spencer Stuart, demonstrated that an inside candidate is the best choice for CEO in a well-performing organization. Conversely, an outsider is the best choice in a company in poor health and in need of a turnaround.[2]

Apple is again a great example of a company that had the right CEO at the right time. As we will discuss in more detail in the next chapter, Steve Jobs returned to Apple in mid-1997 as Interim CEO, at a time when the company was considered to be "a struggling Silicon Valley icon" according to *Wired*,[3] with a stock price that was only $3.42 per share. Six months later Apple had returned to profitability, and its stock price was $25.70 per share by the end of 1999. Jobs officially became CEO in January 2000, and the company began releasing a series of innovative products. Due to Jobs' vision and innovation, by August 2011, the company's stock price had risen to more than $350 per share and Apple was considered to be the most valuable company in the world, with millions of its products sold around the globe.[4]

The opposite is true as well, as the designation of the *wrong* CEO can substantially harm a company. The Los Angeles County Medical Association (LACMA) has had the highest number of CEO turnovers of any of my clients. During an 11-year period, they have had eight people serve as CEO, Interim CEO, or Consultant with executive authority. With so much change in the top executive spot, it was no surprise to me that LACMA's membership statistics and financial strength were very poor when compared to other county medical societies around California. In fact, LACMA's parent organization, the California Medical Association (CMA), established a review group to look into LACMA's difficulties. The review group recommended that LACMA streamline its numerous districts in order to become more efficient, and a new CEO is now in place, charged with making LACMA more meaningful to physicians in Los Angeles. Having the right leader at the helm is essential for organizational success.

Not only do the right people have to be on the leadership team at the beginning of the transformation process; they must also be in the right positions throughout the company to execute the transformation. That means that positions need to match the individual strengths, and other members of the team need to cover individual weaknesses. Results will be suboptimal if an employee is in a position that does not utilize his or her strengths. This is precisely why initial employment interviews must accurately assess strengths and weaknesses, so that organizations can make a good hire and put the right person in the right position from the very beginning.

## Motivating Others

It is important to understand your own personal motivators when you're trying to determine how to motivate other people. When I ask my audiences what compels them to give their all to a specific assignment, the number-one thing they cite is the leader—the person who has given the assignment. An inspirational leader will stir people to perform much better than an uninspired one.

Employees aren't likely to perform optimally if they feel their leader is dumping an unwanted task on them. Similarly, if they feel they're being micromanaged by a leader who tells them exactly what to do and when, they'll most likely feel resentment and think (but not say out loud): "Well, then why don't you do it yourself?" Leaders who are perceived as unappreciative, harsh, or unfair in their criticism will incite resentment in employees, who will then underperform.

Everyone on the planet is motivated when they feel that others appreciate them. This is what makes recognition and rewards so very important; and they don't have to be elaborate or extravagant. It might be just a simple thank-you note (handwritten is best), a write-up and photo in the company newsletter (with the names spelled correctly), or an award at a company dinner. You can use some of the rewards you listed in Chapter 7, or if funds are available, other more expensive rewards can include pay raises, bonuses, educational perks with offsite travel, and celebrations.

At one of the leadership programs I conducted for the Massachusetts Medical Society, a Past President raised his hand and said. "Dr. Reynolds, don't forget to mention food!" A good meal, of course, is an excellent motivator—not only in terms of providing nourishment, but also camaraderie among co-workers. (And it's best if it is more than a box lunch with a sandwich and a bag of chips—unless, of course, you're at the company picnic.)

Some studies cite that people who like a certain event or undertaking will tell many fewer people about it than if they *dislike* the event or undertaking. One estimate is that bad reports outnumber good reports by 200 to 1.[5] In short, bad news travels faster and farther than good news. If employees feel that managers have mistreated or failed to recognize them for their hard work, they will most likely tell a lot of people, thereby undermining the leader's effectiveness. It is especially important for a leader who works with volunteers to avoid criticizing them if at all possible. Instead, if they find a weakness, the best approach is to maximize the volunteer's strengths and have another volunteer cover the weakness so that negative comments do not spread.

Another important motivator is for the employees to have passion for the work and feel a common sense of purpose about the assignment. They need to feel that the task is worth doing and possible to complete given the resources, time, and money available to them. It also helps if both the work and the people involved in the assignment are fun. Employees need to feel empowered to do the assignment, using their skills and creativity to solve the problem within the guidelines the leader gives.

Money and benefits are usually strong motivators—the exception is in organizations that rely heavily on volunteers, such as professional associations. Flexibility is a key motivator when working with volunteers, since they generally want to complete their assignments in their own free time. However, everyone involved in the project must agree upon deadlines, and leaders must always provide guidance along the way.

## Coaching to Improve Performance

Adequate training is a must when employees join a company or change positions within that company. It's also wise to provide coaching for new hires or for underperformers. Most of the coaching I have done has been with physicians, either those who are not meeting certain quality standards or those who have demonstrated disruptive behavior towards other physicians or hospital personnel.

Executive coaching has been around for a long time and has been proven to be effective. In one study conducted by executive coaching firm Manchester, coaching provided a five-to-one return on investment for coaching dollars spent.[6] But while CEOs and other C-suite executives understand the benefits that coaching can provide, physicians tend to be independent thinkers; they're usually very self-assured, and often do not see any need for a coach.

As one of the very first physician coaches, I therefore learned some lessons that are applicable for coaches in any profession or industry. First, it is important to build rapport. If you can't achieve this crucial first step, then another coach should be used. Second, coaching must be confidential, since this relationship is built on trust. The person being coached has to understand that the coach's job is to help him or her be more successful. The only way a coach succeeds is if the coachee succeeds. In effect, these two are joined at the hip as they work together to improve performance and bring more success.

You cannot see coaching as a short-term fix; rather, it has to be a long-term engagement. People can learn new behaviors relatively quickly once they're made aware of what the expectations are. But it takes time to make new behaviors into ingrained habits. My most successful coaching engagements have a weekly or biweekly coaching session in the first month or two, and then have check-ups at 3 months, 6 months, and sometimes 9 months and 12 months to make sure the behavior has become a habit and that participants haven't returned to their old ways.

Short-term coaching assignments usually bring some improvement. This was the case with a physician client of mine, whose charting was insufficient for hospital coders to maximize reimbursement from Medicaid. His charting improved greatly and reimbursement rose after only one session. The CEO was very pleased—so pleased that he moved me to another assignment after just one month of improvement, in spite of my objection. Afterwards, the physician I had coached did what any human being would do: He went back to his old charting behavior within a month or so because the behavior had not become a habit.

The saying that a picture says a thousand words has proven to be a very effective coaching tool for my work with physicians. After all, no physician ever wanted to be at the bottom of the class. If their quality data or length-of-stay statistics are below expectations, just showing them where they stand in relation to their peers (in an anonymous manner) frequently provides the impetus for improvement. Of course the data must be relevant, accurate, and timely.

Physicians will always challenge the data. For example, the most common complaint I hear from physicians when looking at length-of-stay data is that their patients are sicker than other physicians' patients, and therefore have to be in the hospital longer. If this is the case, it is important to compare apples to apples when coaching to improve performance. In other words, you need to compare the person being coached to his or her peer group.

I learned the importance of comparing apples to apples when I worked with a nephrologist who ran a dialysis unit, but whose length-of-stay data was longer than expected. He said he was being compared to all of the internists on the hospital's medical staff, and therefore the data was not fair. Since I agreed that his patients definitely *were* sicker than most of the internal medicine patients, I told him that I would get data for his peer group—only the seven nephrologists who also had dialysis patients. He thought that was much fairer. And even after reviewing the data on the graph I gave him, he could see that his numbers were not as good as his true peers. He went on to make a couple of appropriate changes in his practice, and his numbers improved.

Timely data is necessary for change to occur. At a leadership meeting at one of my client hospitals, the marketing director showed beautiful color-coded charts that displayed each doctor's quality performance results by color and letter of the alphabet rather than by name. His pictures made it obvious which doctors fell off the bell-shaped curve for each treatment measured. When asked what he was going to do with the data, he said he would get new data in a year and show it again at next year's leadership meeting. He didn't seem to realize that behavioral change is unlikely to occur after waiting an entire year and may only be temporary, even if it does. People need to see the numbers much more frequently in order for them to have an impact. Showing data every month or at least quarterly has proven to be quite effective in motivating lasting change.

Coaching to improve measurable outcomes such as quality or length-of-stay data is relatively easy, and may only require a small amount of advice or education plus quarterly check-ups. But coaching someone with behavioral problems, like yelling and screaming at staff, is much more challenging. The most important part of this type of coaching assignment is the initial assessment. You need to ask questions that uncover triggers and help you get to the bottom of the situation. For example, might the person have underlying issues, such as narcissistic personality disorder, which will benefit more from psychiatric care rather than coaching? I learned when studying psychiatry as a medical student, that while you can change a behavior, you absolutely cannot change someone's personality.

I've found that it takes longer to correct a bad behavior problem than a practice pattern problem in coaching physicians. These sorts of assignments run for a year or more, and there are no charts or graphs to show the coachee. Instead, regular feedback and rewards for good behavior are helpful. Money talks, too; so some of my hospital clients have the difficult physician pay my coaching fees, but offer to pay back at least half if the physician demonstrates good behavior for one year.

## Mentoring Generation Y

One offshoot of coaching is mentoring. The word *mentor* comes from Homer's *Odyssey*; specifically, the character Mentor,

Odysseus' friend whom he trusted to look after and educate his son, Telemachus, while he was away. According to *Webster's Dictionary*, a mentor is "a trusted friend and advisor." In his book *Managers as Mentors*, author Chip Bell calls mentoring "that part of a leader's role that has learning and growth as its primary outcome."[7] Mentoring differs from teaching in that it not only includes the exchange of knowledge, but it also has the goal of helping the mentee be successful in his or her career, as well as in life.

It is important to note that the generation born after the mid-1980s wants mentors as they enter the workforce. Generation Y has its own unique set of attributes when compared with Baby Boomers and Generation X, since Gen Yers grew up in an era during which parents stopped spanking and disciplining harshly and began coaching and building self-esteem. They face threats such as 9/11 and global warming, which seem more immediate than the atomic bomb and the Cold War. They prefer a more casual work environment, and a culture that is far less hierarchical than that which previous generations built. Their attendance in company activities can be spotty, as they have a much higher degree of focus on work-life balance. They usually consider attendance at a daughter's soccer game on a Saturday morning more important than golf with a company executive or business partner.

Gen Yers also want their rewards now, not at the end of their careers. This is due in part to the much higher debt load they bear when entering the job market, the significantly higher cost of housing, and a sense of uncertainty about what the future holds for them. Mentors need to customize career development plans and incentives to fit their mentees' needs, and keep in mind that Gen Yers expect their companies to be loyal to *them* rather than the other way around.

The most successful mentoring relationships are partnerships, and are equal rather than hierarchical in nature. They are based on trust, honesty, and interdependence. The relationship might be short-term—perhaps lasting only a year or two—and focused on a specific set of issues; or, it might last longer, evolving to the point that the roles of mentor and mentee occasionally reverse.

## Building an Effective Team

As the quote at the beginning of this chapter says, teams can accomplish a lot more than an individual working alone. While building an effective team can be a challenge, once again, the most important factor is getting the right people in the right positions. A key element in building a team is trust—in both the leader and in and amongst team members. Each team member needs to know for certain that everyone on the team, including him or herself, will be giving their best effort to the assigned task. If just one person fails to do his or her part, the team cannot function at peak performance—even if all the other team members are doing their best.

In sports, for example, team members' strengths needs to match their positions, while their weaknesses need to be covered by others on the team. For example, I learned from watching the movie *The Blind Side* that the offensive left tackle on a football team has a key role in protecting the right-handed quarterback when he steps back and turns to the right to throw a pass. As he turns, the quarterback cannot see what is coming at him on his left side—his blind side. Therefore, that is his weakness. It is the job of the left tackle, whose strength is sheer brawn and athleticism, to cover the quarterback's weakness and prevent him from being sacked.

I have found in my consulting work that balancing personality types in any given workgroup or team is a key ingredient for success. I have used the PACE® Color Palette, a screening tool that uses four colors to determine basic personality traits, at several of my leadership workshops. It is basically a quick, simplified version of the well-known Myers-Briggs personality test.

The test defines red personalities as those who are action-oriented, energetic, spontaneous, and fun, but who might work too quickly and get sloppy. They tend to have lower attention to detail. Yellow personalities are very process-oriented, focused on details, and may drive reds crazy with all their planning, agendas, policies, and procedures. Yellows also run the risk of getting stuck or bogged down with their processes. Blue personalities are nice people who like to build consensus and make everyone happy. They are good listeners and are easy to get along with. But since they hate conflict so much, they tend to be slow to make decisions, because it takes time to get consensus from everyone without hurting anyone's feelings. Green personalities are creative, out-of-the-box thinkers who are focused on strategy but who tend to work alone.

Ideally, every workgroup should have a balance of all four personality types. This allows creative ideas to surface (green), a drive towards action to take place (red), a process for execution to be established (yellow), and a consensus that is easy to build (blue). By providing this balance, you maximize the group's success. But if just one component is missing, you risk having a lack of a creative ideas (no green), reduced forward action (no red), less attention to details or order (no yellow), or weak camaraderie or agreement (no blue).

I conducted this PACE® exercise several years ago with the leaders of the American Society of Plastic Surgeons. I found the group to be visual learners in a prior NLP exercise I had conducted—and additionally discovered that they loved the colors. They decided that personality balancing was so important that they would use the PACE® Color Palette to test all the physicians who wanted to serve on any of their many national committees.

Another aspect of building an effective team is maintaining ongoing communication. Returning to the football game example, the offensive team huddles after nearly every play to communicate the next play, constantly updating the team strategy as they move the ball down the field. Regular communication is absolutely necessary for team success, as well as for a team to function at peak performance. If even one team member does not know what the others are doing—and what support they may need—the group as a whole becomes much less efficient.

In his book *Leading Change*, author John Kotter explains how extremely important it is to use every means possible to communicate any change initiative throughout the organization.[8] He also makes it clear that the best method to use depends on the organization's culture. Some companies are phone cultures, where people pick up the phone, talk to each other, or leave voicemails. A growing number of organizations are switching to email or texting culture as smartphones increase in popularity and younger people, who use them so frequently, enter the workforce.

It is also important to copy the right people when sending out memos. If people did not get the memo—either because they were not on the cc list, or because someone left a phone message and they only check their email—they will feel excluded, and resentment can build.

There is one more point of caution if you find yourself in an email culture. People can seriously misunderstand emails at times, since it's a method of interaction that only uses written words. As we mentioned in Chapter 6, this represents only about 7 percent of what individuals are actually communicating because it omits vocal tone and body language. It is far too easy to cause confusion and ruffle feathers because someone misinterprets an email's tone. For example, someone who uses all caps in an email may come across as angry, although their intent might have only been to add emphasis. Or, someone could miss the main point because it's hidden in a lengthy email that they've merely skimmed. If a multiple paragraph email receives only a one-word reply (such as "OK"), the sender may feel slighted, assuming the receiver didn't take the time to appreciate the thought they put into the message. This is precisely why important messages are best delivered in person. This allows you to see someone's body language, hear his or her tone of voice, and appreciate the full meaning of what he or she is communicating.

# Invest in People

A crucial step in developing your workforce is to invest in people. Employees may benefit from additional education and training as the marketplace in certain industries change. One of my clients, Northeast Georgia Health System, was facing a major shift in the healthcare industry and knew that physician leadership would be a key factor in their future success. They therefore decided to invest in a two-year physician leadership training program with my company so that, as the CEO put it, "a critical mass of physician leaders" would have the knowledge and skills they would need to better align with the hospital during a time of transformational change.

An organization that invests in learning and growth in this way often enjoys a more collaborative culture. Those who receive additional training feel that their company values them, as long as they are not forced to take a course in which they have no interest. Employees must see training as a benefit, one that will help advance their own careers within the organization.

A cultural change usually takes place when a company transforms itself. However, this kind of alteration does not occur overnight; therefore, education and ongoing training are key elements in speeding up the process. As we mentioned in Chapter 4, both company purpose and core values provide a sense of corporate identity, while Chapter 6 cited the importance of establishing a compelling vision. Changes in those elements require leaders to communicate regularly, throughout the company, so that the new key concepts become ingrained in the corporate identity and strategy.

The healthcare industry as a whole is undergoing a cultural change to improve patient safety in hospital settings. Based on changes in the airline industry and a study from the Institute of Medicine entitled, "To Err is Human"[9] the culture is shifting away from "blame and shame" of an individual when a medical error occurs to a culture of systems analysis and education to prevent further errors from occurring in the future.

This cultural shift is especially hard to achieve in healthcare due to the frequency of medical malpractice suits against physicians and hospitals. However, most hospitals have instituted ongoing training programs for physicians and hospital staff that emphasize the need to take the following actions:

1. Prevent patient error through systems analyses that look for the root cause of the error.
2. Use checklists before procedures, analogous to what pilots use in the cockpit before takeoff.
3. Develop patient safety initiatives such as "slip-and-fall" prevention protocols.
4. Provide mechanisms for confidential reporting so that no error goes unanalyzed.

Thanks to these measures, the culture is slowly, but surely, shifting.

## The Power of Rewards

As mentioned earlier, rewards can be great motivators. When used appropriately, they can help build team spirit and inspire groups to give their best effort. An excellent example of the power of rewards to motivate a team to perform with maximum effort is the TV show *Survivor*. In each episode of this show, two tribes (their term for team) compete for a reward, usually a great meal in a beautiful location perhaps accompanied by local entertainment or a much needed shower and massage. Since food and accommodations are at a bare minimum when the tribes are at their camps, this reward is a major luxury. All tribe members are motivated to give their very best effort. If one slips up, he or she is often voted out of the tribe shortly thereafter, so that stronger tribe members can compete in the next reward challenge three days later.

Because of the TV show's popularity, I have used the *Survivor* format in some of my programs to liven up topics that might otherwise be quite dry. One such subject is the latest Accreditation Standards for Hospitals from The Joint Commission, which are updated every year. To make the subject more palatable to my physician audiences, I split them up into tribes. They choose tribe names and wear colored bandanas to signify unity. Then they take a pre-test about The Joint Commission to see how much they know already. After that, they listen to a lecture containing the didactic information they need to learn. Then, to see how much they have retained, the tribes take a post-test, complete with bonus questions at the end for extra credit. Then the scores are tallied and prizes are given, usually something simple like Starbucks cards or a book on leadership. The dollar amount of the prize must fall well within Stark regulations about how much a physician can receive from a hospital.

Three things usually happen whenever I hold this competition with physicians. First there is outright competition from the very beginning, perhaps an inherent personality trait of physicians. Second, most attendees retain a great amount of the material taught in the didactic portion of the program. Third, usually one or two doctors in the room are fairly knowledgeable, even at the beginning. That doctor's teammates have to rely on him or her for the pre-test, so team collaboration—not necessarily an inherent physician trait—is crucial. It is also obvious who does not know much about the subject initially, and those are the physicians who tend to know the most at the time of the post-test. By making the teaching method fun, a great deal of learning can occur.

## Physical Assets

This chapter has focused thus far on people and changing the culture of your organization. However, as we mentioned in Chapter 1, the physical aspect of an organization includes more than just its people; it also includes physical assets such as bricks and mortar, equipment, and finances. You must also consider these physical assets in transforming your organization—especially if they rated poorly on your organizational assessment in Chapter 3.

Of course, all of the physical assets are interconnected. When facilities are not well maintained, staff morale can suffer. Customers who visit on site may express concern about the corporate image and decide to take their business elsewhere. Sometimes all that is needed is a fresh coach of paint and some new furniture or wall hangings to brighten the work atmosphere. Other situations might require more extensive renovations to present a better public image and to make the workspace more conducive to teamwork and a collaborative environment.

Technological advances necessitate equipment updates on a regular basis, which can be a costly undertaking that substantially impacts an organization's finances. But staff frustration and even anger can grow when computers crash, the phone system malfunctions, or other equipment breaks down. At a minimum, you should have adequate tech support and regular equipment maintenance check-ups to prevent such equipment failures and the accompanying employee discontent. You also need to have a budgeting process in place to upgrade or replace equipment over time. Without such a plan, you could end up having to purchase several new pieces of expensive equipment at the same time, potentially causing a financial shortfall.

Finances are often the presenting problem, the chief complaint in an organization. But rarely does an influx of cash, perhaps from a business loan or an investor, solve the underlying problem. An important remedy is for companies to carefully monitor the revenue cycle, making sure it is not too long and that the days of cash on-hand are adequate. When staff morale drops due to other causes, there may even be a problem with misappropriation of company funds. Financial controls and regular internal audits to make sure all funds are accounted for can help to spot and rectify these kinds of situations.

More often than not, a financial problem is a symptom of an underlying problem with Purpose, Passion, Planning, or People. By diagnosing the causative issues and treating them with some of the suggestions made in previous chapters, your organization's financial situation will likely improve.

Rainy days do happen, and events out of your control may cause your organization to have an unexpected shortage of cash. Therefore, it is essential that you have an established process for assuring that adequate reserves are always on hand. You may invest some of these reserves based on the advice of an investment professional. Because the stock market has been very unpredictable in recent years, my advice is to be very conservative in your investment strategy for these funds.

Up to this point, we have discussed how Purpose, Passion, Planning, and People can transform your organization. But how can you sustain your success? The next chapter will present a 5th P—Perseverance—which is the ultimate key for lasting success. We will then provide you with a road map for putting all of the lessons in this book together. But first, here is your prescription for success that highlights the key points in this chapter.

## The Prescription: Developing People, Transforming Your Culture

1. Human capital is a valuable corporate asset; however, it has to be the right human capital, meaning that you've put the right people in the right positions.
2. An inspiring leader can best motivate a team. Rewards are powerful motivators.
3. For a coach to be successful, the coachee must succeed.
4. Generation Y has different values and work ethics than previous generations. They want mentors in a partnership rather than teachers in a hierarchical relationship.
5. When building a team, it is best to match team members' strengths with the positions they are in. You can then cover each team member's weakness with another team member's strength. Personality testing can be used to balance a team or workgroup.
6. Conduct your most important communications in person rather than by e-mail or by phone.
7. Invest in human capital. Changing a culture takes time, and education and ongoing training will speed up the process.
8. Determine if your facility is in need of a face-lift, and make appropriate improvements that fit within your budget.
9. Make sure you have adequate tech support and equipment maintenance personnel to handle equipment failures in a timely manner. Budget well in advance for equipment upgrades or replacement needs.
10. Assure that you have adequate financial systems in place to maximize top-line revenue and cash flow, control expenses, and have adequate reserves. Provide internal auditing mechanisms to prevent mismanagement of funds.

# Making Success Last: The 5th P, Perseverance

*I do not think there is any other quality so essential to success of any kind as the quality of perseverance. It overcomes almost everything, even nature.*

—John D. Rockefeller

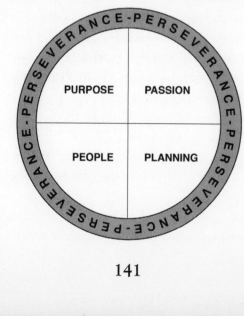

I've written this book to present the model I developed for diagnosing and treating what ails companies—a model that is analogous to what I use to diagnose and treat my patients. Specifically, I use the 4 Ps—Purpose, Passion, Planning, and People—to initially assess and transform the organization. However, I have discovered that there also has to be a 5th P—namely, Perseverance—in order to achieve lasting success. Transformation can occur without it, but will not be sustained over the long run.

## The 5th P: Perseverance

Having been born on Abraham Lincoln's birthday, I have always had a fascination with his life and accomplishments. I have also been amazed and inspired by how he managed to succeed in spite of a long track record of political defeats, business failures, and personal tragedies. As chronicled in David Herbert Donald's biography *Lincoln*, the man who became the 16th President of the United States, lost his mother at the age of nine.[1] He ran for the Illinois State Legislature in 1832, but lost. He opened a general store with a partner the next year, but the business had failed by the end of the year, leaving Lincoln in debt for several years. The woman he loved, Ann Rutledge, died in 1835. He subsequently suffered a serious episode of depression. He was unsuccessful in his attempt to win a seat in Congress in 1843, and though he was elected in 1846, served only one term. He was devastated when his son Edward died in 1850 before his fourth birthday. He lost his bid for a seat in the United States Senate in 1855. He ran for Vice President in 1856 and lost. He was defeated again when he ran for the Senate against Stephen A. Douglas in 1858. With such a dismal history of loss, how did he become President of the United States in 1860—and not just any President, but one of the greatest Presidents we have ever had?

One word comes to mind: Perseverance, the 5th P in the Prescription for Lasting Success. According to *Webster's Dictionary*, to *persevere* means "to persist in the pursuit of an end or enterprise undertaking in spite of counterinfluences, opposition, or discouragement." *New York Times* writer David Brooks notes in a January 12, 2012 column entitled "The C.E.O in Politics" that "great leaders have often experienced crushing personal setbacks."[2] They have the ability to overcome adversity, showing resilience against the odds and in the face of defeat. In short, they persevere. This description seems to describe Lincoln to a tee.

My own experiences have certainly taught me the importance of the old adage, "If at first you don't succeed, try, try again." I have had to reinvent myself on several occasions, most dramatically as a result of Mother Nature's impact on my life and business during the mid-1990s. At the forefront, though, has always been my commitment to developing physician leaders so that they have the knowledge and skills necessary to transform the U.S. healthcare system.

As I was beginning to write this chapter, I found an old copy of *Learning to Lead* by Warren Bennis and Joan Goldsmith.[3] In it I found an exercise that I had filled out more than a decade ago, in which my vision was to create a professional development center for physicians in California. From the strategy map I filled out in the book, it was clear that the institute I eventually created was in its embryonic stage at that time—a mere concept with potential partners in the AMA and the CMA. And I *did* create a physician leadership development institute for the AMA, and conducted joint programs with the AMA and the CMA based on that initial vision.

However, that version of the institute proved to be short-lived, lasting less than two years. Although I was worried when the AMA spun it off, I knew the market and understood there was a huge need I could fill. I stuck with my *Purpose*, was *Passionate* about my vision, put a *Plan* of action in place, and found the right *People* to help me develop my own organization: The Institute for Medical Leadership.® Same concept . . . different formulation. I kept going. I persevered.

I knew it would be important as I got my own institute up and running to get the right people on board—first in terms of faculty, and then in administrative support positions. I also found out quickly that not all of the initial people were the right people, and that some were in the wrong positions. Some have changed positions since we began so that I maximize their strengths and cover their weaknesses.

Some business relationships have come and gone, and I have had to rethink some of our services and programs in order to adjust to the ever-changing healthcare marketplace. But our purpose has remained essentially constant: We've always sought to develop physician leaders so that they can have a significant impact in transforming the U.S. healthcare system.

In his latest book, *Great by Choice*, author Jim Collins tells the story of two teams of explorers who started out for the South Pole at around the same time in 1911.[4] Only one team, led by Roald Amundsen, made it successfully to the pole and then safely home. All members of the second team, led by Robert Scott, perished in the heavy winter storms at the pole. Though both groups faced the same weather conditions, they used different strategies to approach daily progress. Amundsen's group took a slow and steady approach, aiming to travel 20 miles every single day, whether or not the weather favored a faster pace or posed a major obstacle to moving forward. Scott's team sped up on good days but held back on bad days, thereby making very little progress. Though it would have been easy to speed up when the weather was good, the Amundsen team chose not to because they knew they needed all of their energy to persevere and keep going—even on the bad days. In the end, the slow and steady approach proved to be not only successful, but also literally life-saving.

How do you know if you should keep going in the direction you are going, or if you should abandon what you have been working on? Passion is a key clue here. If you continue to feel passion for your mission and vision, keep going; but be realistic. Your timing might be off, or you might have the right people in the wrong positions. Maybe you currently lack the resources you need to make your vision a reality. If you feel stalled in your endeavor, adding the 5th P, Perseverance, to the basic 4 Ps of Purpose, Passion, Planning, and People can help you determine your next steps. You also need to have a renewal process in place for assessing your organizational health on a regular basis, which we'll discuss in more detail below.

I was struck by a Successories poster about perseverance that said,

> *"The difference between history's boldest accomplishments and its most staggering failures is often, simply, the diligent will to persevere."*

Having patience and the right timing can be critical to success when the going gets tough. You may have a great idea and a sound strategy, but a downturn in the marketplace may necessitate a delay in releasing a new product or service. While you don't have control over certain external forces, being able to predict how to be in the right place, at the right time, with the right product or service is crucial for continued success.

## Elements of Perseverance

My experience in establishing The Institute for Medical Leadership® has taught me that there are four essential elements of perseverance: commitment, focus, endurance, and an ongoing renewal process. Anyone who has ever tried to lose weight, for example, knows that commitment to a weight loss regimen is essential for success. Pounds can come off with a healthy diet and regular exercise. But those pounds will come back on (with a few more, as well!) without a sustained commitment to the weight-loss goal.

This element of commitment to a specific goal or objective must also be present in organizations. Unless you commit deeply to reaching a desired goal, it becomes very easy to wander off track or fall short of the mark. Something new might catch your interest and you opt to pursue that goal—leaving the original goal behind, unattained. I never lost sight of my goal in developing The Institute, which is why and how it has become a lasting reality.

Focus is also a key element of perseverance. Becoming too scattered might cause you to get distracted and fail to persevere in reaching your stated goals. Using the weight-loss analogy again, let's say that you decide to start your diet with Weight Watchers, but then see an enticing ad for Jenny Craig. You switch to the Jenny Craig meal plan, but then think you could combine the two approaches on your own. In the end, you'll have lost focus on one proven success strategy, and your self-designed program will most likely fail.

My focus at The Institute has always been on physician leaders and the healthcare industry. Since many leadership skills are trans-ferrable, other professionals—including lawyers, engineers, and insurance people—have asked us to teach these same skills to their groups. However, I have always felt that widening the scope of our work to include other industries would dilute our focus and cause us to spread ourselves too thin. I worry that we'll then accomplish less. So although we do accept most assignments that come in regardless of the industry, our marketing efforts remain targeted on our true area of expertise: the healthcare industry.

Medical societies and other volunteer organizations can have significant problems with commitment and focus due to their frequently changing leadership. A new President is elected every year or two. That person has often worked his or her way up a leadership ladder from committee Chair, to Treasurer, to Secretary, to Vice President, to President-elect, and finally to President. This climb to the top may take 6 to 10 years, depending on the lengths of the terms for each position.

On the way up the leadership ladder, many future Presidents develop strong opinions about what key issue or pet project they want to tackle during their presidential year. That means that there is a new focus, a new project to work on, and most likely a dilution of the goals and objectives in the organization's strategic plan every year. There may not be enough time, talent, or treasure to complete the President's project within a year. Additionally, shifting the organization's focus every year can be quite taxing on the staff.

A friend of mine who was a medical society executive director once told me that his greatest challenge was having "a new boss every year." And every year, that new boss wanted to change the organization's focus, diverting valuable staff and resources away from the organization's core purpose, vision, and strategic goals. It comes as no surprise that this organization accomplished much less than desired because of this lack of focus and diluted commitment.

Endurance—performing over the long haul even in the face of difficulties—is also a necessary component of perseverance. In spite of adverse events or large obstacles in your way, you must be able to continue your forward progress as the Amundsen team did on their successful round trip to the South Pole—even against the odds. Many Americans make a New Year's resolution to lose weight, and opt to join a gym to get more exercise. But fitness industry research shows that within only six weeks of toughing it out on the treadmill and other exercise equipment, 60 percent of people forget their resolution and stop going to the gym. Clearly lacking endurance, they return to their comfortable couches at home instead.[5]

## The Importance of Renewal

Enduring adverse situations require an ongoing renewal process to keep you and your team as fit and able as possible to ride out any storms that come your way. Without renewal, frustration will set in, people may feel overwhelmed, and burnout can occur, thus stalling any forward progress toward your goal. Returning to our weight-loss example, we know that plateaus can occur along the way to the final target. It is crucial to maintain your commitment, keep your focus on the goal, endure your feelings of frustration, *and* have a plan of self-care (renewal) that will see you through those plateaus. An excellent strategy for ultimate success includes advance planning of activities you enjoy—provided they do not sabotage your weight-loss efforts. When regularly scheduled, these things can help you stay on track by providing opportunities for self-renewal.

I learned my lesson about the need for renewal the hard way when the Malibu Emergency Room closed. I had not taken care of myself, and had instead become entirely consumed with running the emergency center with all its inherent stresses. I had taken on way too many volunteer activities, and was working a second shift as a wife and mother at the end of very taxing days. What I valued most was my family, but I had become trapped in a "life-saving" mindset, telling myself that "my patients need me"—not realizing that they most needed me to remain *well*. I ended up being completely burned out and exhausted—and with no renewal process in place, my life began to crumble around me.

With my external world falling apart, I was forced to turn inward and began meditating on a daily basis at a meditation park near my home. I developed a spiritually based rejuvenation process and gradually felt myself becoming renewed, balanced, and back in sync with the world. I learned during this process that we healers are especially prone to burnout. We give everything we have to others—our caring and compassion, our knowledge and experience, our time and energy—but we often forget to do the same for ourselves. Regular self-renewal is a must if we want to persevere and continue to provide the best care possible for our patients.

Stephen Covey's 7th Habit cites the need for personal renewal, but organizational renewal is equally important. Author John Gardner cites several important benefits of organizational renewal, including: "To renew or reinterpret values, and to create new ones;" "To liberate energies that have been imprisoned by outmoded procedures and habits of thought;" and "To reenergize or to generate new goals appropriate to new circumstances."[6] Rekindling old or creating new energy is essential for organizations to prosper and grow.

As your organization works towards the goals and objectives it has set during the planning process, it must also make sure that burnout does not occur. Again, advance planning of rewards and fun activities that reinvigorate your team and reignite their passion will help keep them on track, committed, focused, and with enough stamina to endure difficulties that arise.

## Building versus Maintaining

Maintenance can be the toughest challenge an individual or a company faces, especially during difficult times. As I have learned on more than one occasion, the hardest thing in any weight-loss program is weight maintenance after you hit your target weight. A firm initial commitment and the best-laid plans are easily forgotten when other things in life intervene. Thus, perseverance is the only way your personal success will be long-lasting.

Maintaining growth at the organizational level can be very difficult, as it may require a new skill set among the leadership ranks. The leader who is at the helm during the growth phase may have the personality traits of a builder rather than a maintainer. He or she may be more interested in creating new things and might not find it challenging to maintain the status quo, even if profits may be stable or increasing. Leaders who achieve initial success may get bored and seek new opportunities at other companies that are more in need of their entrepreneurial/builder mindset.

This is why it's so important for companies to have a well-thought-out succession plan in place. This allows them to continue to maximize their success on a long-term basis if key leaders depart to pursue new ventures elsewhere. Who will guide the company after an initial successful growth spurt? The current leader may move the company forward, building it to new heights of success, but it can be difficult to sustain original gains at the level that is necessary for long-term success. Alternatively, the organization may require an executive search to find a successor with the right skill set to maintain a company's success to date as well as move it forward.

## The Time Frame Challenge

One of the biggest challenges I have seen in strategic planning is that the time frame for action is much too long. I mentioned earlier that one of my clients even had a 40-year strategic plan! In such a case, or even if the plan covers only 5 or 10 years, the follow-up becomes too sporadic to effectively keep people on track. Some things fall through the cracks and people fail to meet certain goals, thereby limiting long-term success. People responsible for executing a certain element of the plan may lose interest and momentum, as other, more immediate tasks divert their focus.

Certainly the longer the time frame of the strategic plan, the more perseverance is needed. Regular—at least quarterly—check-ups are essential to make sure that everyone involved is making progress toward all of the goals and objectives. Leaders must maintain a high level of enthusiasm for the ultimate corporate vision, and communicate it repeatedly throughout the organization. My best advice is to limit the planning period to two or three years at the most, thereby keeping the plan realistic, maintaining commitment and focus, and keeping the need for endurance to a minimum.

## Perseverance in Business

Chapter 8 cited an excellent example of perseverance from the business world: Steve Jobs's career with Apple. A closer look at his ability to persevere in spite of adversity is quite instructive.[7] Jobs launched Apple Computers in 1976 with partner Steve Wozniak.

By 1980, they were able to take the company public because of their innovative product development. Jobs became a multimillionaire at the age of 25.

In 1983, while Jobs focused on developing the Macintosh computer, he asked PepsiCo's John Sculley to become Apple's CEO. The Mac was introduced in 1984 during a Super Bowl ad—and 70,000 Macs were sold in the first 100 days. However, sales slumped the following year, and Sculley and the Apple board of directors abruptly forced Jobs out of the company. Although he felt he had been fired from the company he had built, Jobs never lost sight of his vision to change the world through personal computing.

The year after leaving Apple, Jobs founded NeXT Computing and also bought George Lucas's computer graphics division. Together, these became Pixar Animation Studios, which is now owned by The Walt Disney Company. At one point during this phase of his life, the *Wall Street Journal* described Jobs as someone who might be able to survive "as a niche player" in the computing industry. On the surface he appeared to be down; but we see as the story unfolds that he was certainly not out. Pixar's 1995 success with the animated film *Toy Story* enabled the company to go public, making Jobs a billionaire.

While Jobs was succeeding with NeXT and Pixar, Apple was not faring well. So the company invited their former leader to return as a "special advisor" in 1996. Jobs went on to become Interim CEO in 1997. The following year, Apple made a profit for the first time in five years. Two and a half years later, in 2000, Jobs became Apple's official CEO. During the 14 years that he was at Apple the second time around, he was able to transform not only that organization and build it into the most valuable company in the world, he was also able to transform the entire computing industry as well as the world of music. Had he not persevered with his vision to change the world, Apple would not be the company that it is today.

When we evaluate Jobs' ability to persevere, we see that he clearly exhibited the essential elements of commitment, focus, and endurance. Jobs was definitely committed to changing the world—to invent the future by "thinking different" as he put it.[8] He focused his time and energy on creating new products that would revolutionize the computer industry, the entertainment industry, and people's lives around the world. In fact, by the time of his death in 2011, his name was on 313 patents.

Jobs obviously had the ability to endure in spite of adversity. Pushed out of Apple by Sculley and the board of directors, he continued to pursue his vision to such an extent that he was able to make a comeback at Apple that was even more dramatic than his departure 11 years earlier.

Jobs developed a renewal process at an early age, pursuing the tenets of Zen Buddhism. According to Jobs' biographer, Walter Isaacson, Jobs followed the practices of Eastern religions throughout his life, including meditative practices that calmed his mind and allowed his intuition to flourish.[9] Without this element, he may have been able to persevere through difficult times, but we can only guess to what extent.

## Assessing Perseverance

You must be brutally honest when assessing your personal ability to persevere as well as your organization's ability to persevere. Understanding the four components of perseverance described earlier can serve as a guide during this evaluation. The following scale from 1 to 10 can help you determine the level of commitment, focus, endurance, and renewal that you have both within yourself and your organization. Remember that the leader's ability to persevere is vital to driving the organization forward towards its goals during difficult times. If you as a leader lack any of these four elements, your organization will suffer, and success—though initially attainable—may not last very long.

## Personal Perseverance Scale

On a scale of 1 to 10 (1 being lowest, and 10 being highest) rate
yourself according to the four elements of perseverance listed below.

1. **Commitment**    1——+—+—+—+—+—+—+—10
                                    5

2. **Focus**    1——+—+—+—+—+—+—+—10
                                    5

3. **Endurance**    1——+—+—+—+—+—+—+—10
                                    5

4. **Renewal**    1——+—+—+—+—+—+—+—10
                                    5

## Organizational Perseverance Scale

On a scale of 1 to 10 (1 being lowest, and 10 being highest) rate your
organization according to each of the four elements of perseverance
listed below.

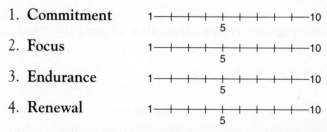

1. **Commitment**    1——+—+—+—+—+—+—+—10
                                    5

2. **Focus**    1——+—+—+—+—+—+—+—10
                                    5

3. **Endurance**    1——+—+—+—+—+—+—+—10
                                    5

4. **Renewal**    1——+—+—+—+—+—+—+—10
                                    5

These simple tallies should give you an idea of where you and
your organization need to make an additional effort in order to
sustain your initial success. Now that you understand where your
perseverance may fall short, here are a few pointers for improving
in the areas that need your attention.

## Improving Commitment

Commitment starts at the top of an organization. If the leaders
are not dedicated to the organization's goals and objectives, it is
unlikely that staff members will follow and execute the strategic
plan in a timely manner. Those who guide the organization must
convey its mission, vision, and core values on a regular basis to

make sure everyone knows why the company is in business, where it is aiming to go, and what it values.

You can evaluate your own level of commitment as a leader by using the process outlined in Chapter 4 to determine if you are in sync with the organization's mission and core values. Do you feel passion for the organization? If not, refer to Chapter 5 to find ways to reignite passion in yourself and then in your organization. Is the corporate vision your own, or is it something you inherited from a predecessor? And do you readily embrace the goals and objectives that make up the strategic plan? If you are not committed to reaching these, then you need to rethink the plan. The process for a strategic transformation summit that is outlined in our final chapter may help you develop a more sustainable one.

## Improving Focus

If your organization seems to lack focus, it's your job as the leader to determine if you need to remove any distractions. Is your planning time frame too long? Are too many goals and objectives diluting the ultimate goal? Are there too many or too few people on the execution team? If, for any reason, staff members don't believe that the goal is attainable, they will most likely give up on it—and move on to something they feel they can realistically accomplish.

An excellent resource for improving focus is a book called *The Power of Focus* by well-known authors Jack Canfield, Mark Victor Hansen, and Lee Hewitt.[10] The book provides 10 "Focusing Strategies," many of which I have found helpful both personally and in business.

## Improving Endurance

It is again the leader who can motivate staff members to endure adversity and weather difficult times. If they don't receive adequate encouragement, people may give up because the odds seem overwhelming. You need to determine what your people can—and cannot—reasonably accomplish. You also need to be the cheer-leader who provides support to your team when things are moving more slowly than anticipated, and keep passion alive for the end vision. Establishing a process of renewal will also help your organization stay in it for the long haul.

You may want to consider hiring an executive coach who can act as advisor and cheerleader as you support your team at work. Having your own support system during difficult times can be invaluable. The coach can serve as your sounding board as you rethink your corporate strategy. If your company seems to be in the doldrums, a coach can motivate you to reignite passion throughout the company, challenging you to move beyond your comfort zone.

## Improving Renewal

Renewal is important not just for your organization, but also for you as the leader. If you are having a bad day, it is unlikely that you can instill passion in your followers to redouble their efforts towards the organization's goals and objectives. You must take time for yourself to renew your body, mind, and spirit. Take a break here and there so that you can relax and get rid of built-up tension. Then, do the same for your organization.

Make sure the renewal process is ingrained in your corporate culture, not just something you do when a crisis has occurred. Giving your staff regular opportunities to rest, relax, and renew will motivate them to tackle even the most difficult challenges with much more stamina than if no renewal process is in place.

The prescription that follows will summarize the key points in this chapter and help you improve your ability to persevere during difficult times. The following (and final) chapter will outline a strategic transformation summit, which pulls all 5 Ps—Purpose, Passion, Planning, People, *and* Perseverance—together to help you maximize your organization's success on a long-term basis.

# The Prescription: Perseverance

1. Assess your personal ability to persevere using the personal perseverance scale in this chapter.

2. Assess your organization's ability to persevere using the organizational perseverance scale in this chapter.

3. Use processes in earlier chapters in this book to strengthen your level of commitment and passion for your organization's mission, core values, vision, and goals and objectives.

   a. Refer to Chapter 4 to reassess your mission and core values.

   b. Refer to Chapter 5 to maximize passion.

   c. Refer to Chapter 6 to create a compelling vision.

   d. Refer to Chapter 7 to develop attainable goals and objectives.

   e. Refer to Chapter 8 to assure your commitment to having the right people in the right positions.

4. Determine if there are distractions that are diluting your organization's focus. Remove any that are impeding forward progress.

5. Provide encouragement to your staff and reiterate the mission, core values, vision, and goals and objectives on a regular basis.

6. Develop a personal renewal process to maximize your ability to endure during difficult times.

7. Consider hiring an executive coach who can provide you with advice and support.

8. Develop an ongoing renewal process that is part of your organization's culture.

# CHAPTER 10

# The Final Prescription: A Strategic Transformation Summit

*The whole is more than the sum of its parts.*

—Aristotle, *Metaphysica*

Now that you have diagnosed what ails your organization and have learned a few methods for treating the areas in need of attention, you may be wondering how to put everything together in a workable manner. After all, it is not enough to come up with new ideas to improve your organization's health; you also need a practical game plan to make lasting success a reality. That is why this final chapter will describe a process you can use on a yearly or biannual basis—a process that uses all 5 Ps presented in this book to maximize your organization's lasting success.

I have attended and facilitated a lot of strategic planning retreats where the goal is to plot an organization's path to success over the following two to five years; however, the word *retreat* always seemed to be a misnomer to me. The word itself means going *backwards*; to retreat is to withdraw, presumably to a safer and quieter position. Strategic planning involves creating a compelling vision and plan of *action* to move *forward* toward the vision, away from the safe and quiet realm of the status quo to a place that helps the organization flourish.

A better phrase is *strategic transformation summit*, which implies reaching *new heights* as your organization undergoes *major change*—rather than just achieving a predetermined goal. The word *summit* is also used when top-level political leaders meet to discuss divisive issues. In this setting, the term implies détente or an easing of tensions between nations. Those involved put aside negative energy so that new strategies and solutions can surface. This is what makes *summit* such an appropriate word for a meeting designed to strategically transform your organization—one that requires you to remove negativity before developing a compelling vision, goals, and objectives.

## Putting All 5 Ps Together

What follows is an outline of a strategic transformation summit that involves all 5 Ps—Purpose, Passion, Planning, People (and other Physical Assets), and Perseverance—which you can use to assess and transform your organization. Please keep in mind that the preparations you make *before* the summit are *as important* as what takes place during the summit. So is ongoing follow-up afterwards. These three elements must work together in order to achieve lasting success.

It is also essential to remember that your organization may only need treatment in one or two areas during this process, not all five. The key is to hone in on the areas that need improvement, while not losing sight of the rest. Always remember to investigate beyond the chief complaint by constantly asking, *"Why?"* Why is revenue down? Why is staff morale low? Why have sales dropped off? Why is your facility in need of repair? If you fail to dig deeper and determine the root cause of the chief complaint, you will only put Band-Aids on the problems, instead of finding the correct treatment plan for long-term success.

## Pre-Summit Preparation

### Step 1: Choose the Right People to Participate in the Summit

As I mentioned earlier, *Good to Great* best-selling author Jim Collins stresses the importance of having "the right people on the bus,"[1] meaning that the choice of the leadership group is paramount to an organization's success. You need to include your best out-of-the-box thinkers, people you are confident will provide independent ideas and critique before, during, and after the summit.

### Step 2: Do an Environmental Scan

The environmental scan is perhaps the most important element of any strategic planning process. Without developing a good understanding of the current marketplace and future trends, any planning process may well miss the mark. You may not understand customer or member needs well enough, and your products and services may well be outdated, obsolete, or irrelevant. Gaining knowledge of your industry's market trends will provide a strong foundation upon which to build your organization's future success.

## Step 3: Do a SWOT Analysis. Identify Key Issues that Need to be Addressed

Ask each summit participant to fill out a SWOT (for strengths, weaknesses, opportunities, and threats) analysis before the summit, identifying their perception of the organization's internal strengths and weaknesses, and the external opportunities and threats it is facing. Then ask them to write down their vision for the organization in the coming three to five years. This preliminary information lets the summit facilitator know if the organization's leadership has divergent views about their company's current capabilities as well as different visions for its future. It also helps decipher what issues need to be addressed during the summit. While you can obtain this information during the summit itself, that takes up valuable summit time that would be better spent on future planning efforts.

I have found it more instructive to get the SWOT information in advance, as the results frequently turn out to be quite surprising. For example, I conducted a recent strategic planning session for a cancer center. The vision statements I received in advance of the program turned out to be far less divergent than the chair thought they had been prior to the meeting. That information let me know that I should shift the meeting's focus away from resolving discord, and instead spend more time helping members develop goals and objectives.

## Step 4: Complete an Organizational Health Assessment

You can also ask all summit attendees to complete the organizational health assessment (see Appendix B) prior to the summit. This assessment will provide information about a company's internal workings, and will usually uncover more detail than the SWOT analysis does. It will also help focus your summit activities on those areas in need of improvement.

## The 5 Ps Summit

### *Introduction: Give an Overview of the 5 Ps Process*

It is crucial for all participants to understand the 5-Ps model in order to maximize the summit's effectiveness. I usually provide a short overview of how the model was developed and then define the 5 Ps: Purpose, Passion, Planning, People and Physical Assets, and Perseverance. I then divide the summit agenda into five sections, each of which covers one of the 5 Ps in sequence.

The length of the summit is important as well. Although I have condensed the program into as little as six hours, it is far more productive to spend a day and a half or two full days working through the steps outlined below. Of course, the length of time you should spend also depends on how healthy your organization is from the get-go. A shorter time frame will suffice if you only have a few issues to address.

### *The 1st P: Purpose and Core Values*

Facilitate a thorough review of your organization's mission statement by asking the group to answer the following questions:

1. What business does the mission statement say you are in?
2. Is that the business that is needed in today's marketplace?
3. Who are your customers or potential customers?
4. Does your current mission statement address their needs?
5. Is your mission statement in sync with your parent organization's mission statement (if you have one)?

6. Does the environmental scan indicate that you might need to alter your mission due to external market forces?

7. How did the group score Purpose on the organizational health assessment? Which questions received the lowest scores?

You might find that you need to adjust your mission statement based on the group's answers to these questions.

The next step is to have the group review your organization's core values. Does everyone in the organization espouse those same core values? Is something missing? If so, what? Are your values in sync with those of your parent company (if you have one)? Do you need to modify any of your current core values?

When the group is in agreement with the organization's Purpose and core values, you can move on to the 2nd P: Passion.

## The 2nd P: Passion

The Passion segment of the summit has two parts. First, I ask all participants what they are currently most excited about in the organization. I may also ask them why they first became involved with the organization or what made them come to work at the company or institution. This exercise reveals what people at the summit are most passionate about.

However, before moving on to the Planning phase of the summit, you have to deal with the 800-pound gorilla in the room, specifically by uncovering: What do people feel the most negative about? Is there something that no one wants to discuss publicly that is limiting the organization's effectiveness? To get to the bottom of this issue, I pass out identical pieces of paper and identical pens, and ask all participants to write down what is bothering them about the company. I then collect the papers and tally the results on a flip chart for all to see.

Occasionally I get a long list of grievances from this exercise that indicates significant problems within the company. But more often,

I will find that only one or two complaints repeatedly appear on several pieces of paper, along with a spattering of others. This is an incredibly effective way to anonymously expose an unresolved issue that is causing turmoil beneath the surface. Once you get it out in the open, you can develop a strategy to deal with it as part of the 3rd P—the Planning process—which the summit participants then address.

For instance, one of my clients discovered through this exercise that many of their department members felt they had very little recognition and clout within their parent institution because of their small size. As part of the goal-setting process, one breakout group worked on strategies to make the department more visible and better understood within the larger institution. Organizations that fail to deal with the 800-pound gorilla usually won't be able to create as compelling a vision or as inspiring a set of goals and objectives, thereby limiting their overall success.

## The 3rd P: Planning—Part 1: Vision

The first part of the Planning phase of the 5-Ps Summit requires that you create a compelling vision for the organization. I use the vision statements the participants wrote down at the end of their SWOT analyses to get some idea about where they think the company should go. I can also determine if a common or unifying vision emerges from those statements.

At the summit itself, I lead a guided imagery exercise in which I ask participants to sit quietly in their chairs with their eyes closed. I then tell them to imagine that it is three years from now and we are all back in the same room. Each of them is giving a report about what the company has done over the past three years, and what the situation is like at that point in the future. I then ask them to bring their attention back into the room in the present day and share what they have envisioned with everyone else. The group then discusses what everyone reports that they imagined taking place in the next three years.

If the organization has a current vision statement, the group can then review it in light of their individual vision statements and what the guided imagery exercise revealed. Is the current vision statement action-oriented and compelling? Does it move the organization forward to what participants have envisioned the future should be? If not, the group should modify the vision statement so they can answer "yes" to these questions. If there is no vision statement at the beginning of the summit, the group works to develop one based on their individual vision statements and the imagery exercise. I recommend that the vision statement be concise, memorable, and compelling.

### The 3rd P: Planning—Part 2: Setting Goals and Objectives

At this point in the summit, I divide participants into three or four small groups with three to six people in each group (depending on the total number of summit participants). I ask each group to focus on topics that have been gleaned from the SWOT analysis, the organizational health assessment, and other pre-summit background information I have gathered from my client. Participants can select which group they want to attend based on their interest and passion for the topic. If there is keen interest in a particular topic, I may hold two group sessions back-to-back so that everyone who is interested can give input about it.

If there is an imbalance in the number of people in the groups, I ask for volunteers to move to another group—again, based on their interest. You don't want a group to have members who aren't interested in their discussion topic because they likely won't propose optimal goals and objectives that move the organization forward.

I give each breakout group 60 to 90 minutes to come up with two to four goals, each with two or three objectives, that address the issue assigned to the group. They must appoint a group leader, a scribe to take notes on a flip chart, and a timekeeper. At the end of the breakout sessions, all of the participants reassemble in the main summit room. Then each group leader reports back to the entire summit about the goals and objectives the group is proposing to address their assigned issue.

When all breakout groups have made their proposal to the whole group, I (as the facilitator) eliminate duplications that may have occurred between the groups' suggestions. Then, the reality check begins: Managers responsible for executing the strategic plan must evaluate how much time, talent, and treasure each proposed goal and objective needs. Time falls under the 3rd P, as part of Planning, while talent and treasure are part of the 4th P, People and Physical Assets.

## Time

Each proposed goal is put on the kind of timeline described in Chapter 7, placing those to be done sooner near the current situation in the bottom-left corner. Goals to be completed later on—closer to the time when they achieve the vision—are placed near the top-right corner. Figure 10.1 shows you this process as a reminder.

### *The 4th P: People and Physical Assets*

Both talent and treasure involve the 4th P—People and Physical Assets—which you should evaluate as described below.

## Talent

The next step is for the facilitator to have summit participants and managers list people or workgroups who will be held accountable for executing each goal and objective according to the timeline. And remember: You do not want to assign these to people who can't accept full accountability because they missed the summit.

## Treasure

Participants are then asked to rate the amount of resources (money, equipment, staff, and any others) necessary for execution as high,

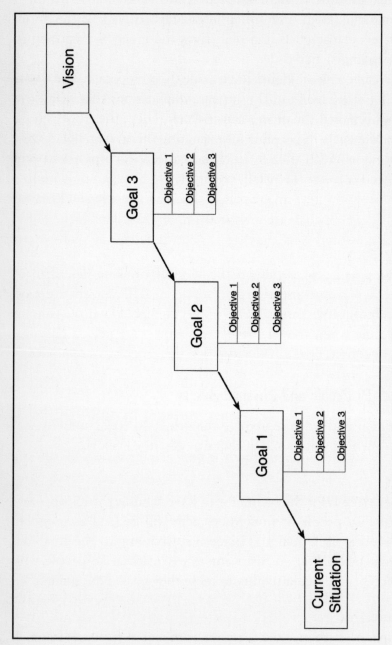

Figure 10.1    Setting a Timeline Working Backwards from the Vision.

medium, or low. They are also asked to rate the amount of time and the number of people involved as high, medium, or low.

## Prioritization

After assessing time, talent, and treasure, summit participants must determine which goals and objectives are doable, and then prioritize them from most to least important. Each participant can vote for their top four or five priorities; you can always include more, depending on the size of the organization and the amount of resources available for plan execution. Higher priorities receive more weight in the voting process. It becomes clear when the votes are tallied which goals are of utmost importance and which, if any, are of little interest to the group as a whole. Goals that do not generate interest should be abandoned.

The final flow chart will include a timeline with the top-priority goals and objectives on it, along with the name of the accountable person or team and a list of the resources needed for each goal and objective. This chart will serve as the ultimate road map for organizational transformation.

## The 5th P: Perseverance

We mentioned earlier that focus is a crucial element of perseverance, which is why I recommend that the final plan have only four or five major goals. A larger number of goals can cause those involved in the execution process to lose concentration and momentum. Each goal will have two to four objectives, since too many objectives can also cloud the picture and diminish focus.

It is also important to establish a regular, ongoing feedback loop to evaluate how much progress you are making toward each goal and objective. Without such feedback, people may put projects aside and miss targets, since no one is checking up. Deadlines may come and go, since there are no consequences to missing them, and people will fall back into the routine of their more familiar responsibilities at the expense of the summit's objectives. In such cases, the entire strategic plan may end up being just another document that takes up space in someone's file drawer, not to be looked at again until a few weeks prior to the next strategic planning meeting two to five years down the road.

The feedback should also include an assessment of what is working and not working, specifically regarding the execution team's strengths and weaknesses. Group members should make adjustments to maximize team strengths and cover weaknesses. Making sure the right people are in the right positions is essential to the success of this feedback process.

There should be an ongoing renewal process that includes meaningful rewards for accomplishing key goals and fun activities to motivate teamwork—especially if the goal or objective is harder to attain than initially realized. A fun event can also reset the level of enthusiasm staff members have for the project at hand, and can also provide a brief, but much needed, respite from a stressful work environment.

You can even use the summit itself to kick off an organizational renewal process. It's a good idea to hold this at an off-site location such as a hotel, country club, or learning center, away from the daily distractions of work like emails, phone calls, and meetings. You can incorporate team-building exercises like good-natured competitions, sporting activities, or parties into the agenda, and even offer leisurely activities or time for inner reflection through yoga or meditation to those who'd like to take advantage of it.

The summit's ultimate goal is to create a healthy organization that is committed to its purpose and core values and has the following characteristics.

- A strong organizational identity that includes service to others.
- Passion felt throughout the organization.
- A compelling vision and workable long-range goals and objectives.

- A culture that develops people and values physical assets.
- A renewal process in place to enable perseverance during difficult times.

All of this will ultimately result in lasting success.

## An Organization in Transformation: The California Medical Association

I have talked throughout this book about organizational transformation that brings lasting success. Transformation means taking a major leap forward rather than simply moving along through linear growth. It implies that members of an organization have created a new vision that propels them to alter the way they've traditionally done business. Such change is not for the faint-hearted, and it does come with some inherent risk. However, the process I have outlined will provide an action plan that minimizes that risk, thereby enabling companies to be bolder in their quest to change the status quo and maximize success over the long run.

One of my clients, the California Medical Association (CMA), is currently undergoing significant transformation. Their example clearly shows how all 5 Ps are moving it forward. Keep in mind as you read about the CMA that organizational transformation does not occur overnight. It takes time, sometimes a lot of time; and not all 5 Ps always need focused attention.

I have been a member of the CMA for nearly three decades and have worked for the organization as a consultant and leadership development trainer for about half of that time. I have witnessed the group's ups and downs as it has gone through several leadership changes at the top of its management structure and its board (which currently has 49 members, and is slated to grow to 54). It has also had several years of financial loss in the recent past.

The most recent change in management occurred at the beginning of 2010 when 35-year-old Dustin Corcoran was named the

CEO. At the time, Mr. Corcoran had worked for the CMA for 12 years; he started as the membership coordinator for the CMA's political action committee, and then worked as a lobbyist for the government relations department. He became Vice President of that department at age 29, after the untimely death of his mentor, Steve Thompson. Due to a subsequent change in CEO, he became a Senior Vice President with responsibilities reaching beyond government relations.

As someone who was able to observe all of these positions internally, Mr. Corcoran developed a deep understanding of structural and cultural problems both within the CMA as well as in its external relationships with its 37 component (county) medical societies. So when he became CEO, he was able to set in motion the elements needed not only to improve, but also to truly transform the organization.

The CMA was founded in 1856 and its mission statement—its Purpose—has been fairly constant throughout that time. Today, it reads as follows:

*"Promoting the science and art of medicine, the care and well-being of patients, the protection of the public health and the betterment of the medical profession."*

However, passion within the organization was an issue; some departments were functioning with positive attitudes and high motivation, while others lagged behind, with low enthusiasm and negative outlooks. In addition, previous management had made some promotions up the ranks without regard to skill or competency, which had lowered overall staff morale.

Mr. Corcoran knew that the culture had to change. He also knew no transformative effort could take hold if he didn't deal with the negative energy that was limiting staff effectiveness.

He therefore decided to work one-on-one with his management team to create a more positive culture. He worked to end negativism, made staffing changes based on meritocracy—meaning that he put the right people in the right positions—and changed several departments' internal structure. No longer are government relations, legal, and regulatory "the Big Three" departments. Instead, the CMA has made a significant investment in communications and marketing, which is now the biggest department. This investment reflects the CMA's renewed focus on its mission, which includes providing much needed two-way communication with physicians in California. Before the CMA expanded this department, many physicians were completely unaware of what the organization had been doing on their behalf.

Mr. Corcoran also noticed a lot of strained relations between some of the county medical societies and the CMA. He knew that he had to dispel this negativity in order for the CMA to move forward. Since becoming CEO, he has been able to build confidence among many county medical society executives in the vision that the CMA can indeed provide management services and back-office support, thereby eliminating duplicate services and a lot of administrative waste. He has proposed that there be no fee for these services, but that each county society instead uses the money they have saved for increased outreach to physicians in that county. Again, the idea of connecting the CMA more directly with California physicians has been an overarching theme.

Mr. Corcoran inherited a strategic planning process from his predecessor, who stayed less than three months in the CEO position. After completing that process, he has focused his efforts on creating a new structure and a positive culture before returning to any sort of formal planning.

He has invested in his people by establishing a fund that will provide staff training and education for all Vice Presidents and, eventually, other staff members, as well. He has used rewards and celebrations as motivators, and notes that the company picnic—an idea that came from a staff member—was a huge success.

When asked about perseverance, Mr. Corcoran says, "The team is doing it." Vice Presidents are bringing new ideas to the table, indicating that the cultural changes are no longer dependent solely on him. Being patient is essential when undergoing a cultural change within an organization, and Mr. Corcoran knows that he must "let the group get there as a group" rather than imposing his will upon them.

The CMA's transformation is still a work in progress that will evolve over the next few months or years. The workforce has already developed a far more positive and cohesive attitude, and staff morale is high. Roger Purdy, CMA Associate Vice President and Program Director of the CMA's Annual Leadership Academy, says, "Although I was skeptical when [Dustin] started, I'm becoming a true believer. . . . There's a fresh new feeling around CMA and a lot of optimism, the likes of which is unprecedented in my 30 years here."

By focusing on transforming structure and culture, Mr. Corcoran was able to return the CMA to financial stability and growth. In fact, the CMA will end the year in the black for the first time in five years. Had he focused only on the chief complaint of financial loss, the organization would not be where it is today.

## Transforming Your Organization

The CMA example shows that while all 5 Ps—Purpose, Passion, Planning, People and Physical Assets, and Perseverance—are part of the transformation process; you don't always need to work on all of them. The key is to look beyond the chief complaint, diagnose what areas need treatment, and provide remedies that will address the presenting problem's underlying cause. You do need to evaluate all 5 Ps as the company begins to transform itself, and reassess them at regular intervals to assure that transformative efforts stay on track and success is long-lasting. And you will no doubt find along the way that Aristotle was right when he said that "the whole is more than the sum of its parts."

Do members of your organization adhere to its purpose and core values throughout the company? Does the workforce exhibit a sense of passion for what they do? Is the vision compelling? Are the strategic goals and objectives inspiring—and doable? Are the right people in the right positions? Do physical assets need attention? Is there an ongoing process of renewal ingrained in the culture that enables perseverance during difficult times?

Whether you use a formal process such as the strategic transformation summit described in this chapter or just use one or two of the prescriptions included in this book, my hope is that you now have more strategies to transform your organization. I also hope that, in the process, some of the strategies will make you a better leader and enable you to bring lasting success to your organization.

# APPENDIX A

# Personal Health Assessment

The following personal health assessment is divided into four sections, each containing 10 statements about one aspect of your health. You are to select the answer that best describes you using a five-point scale ranging from "Always" (5) to "Never" (1). Please rate yourself between 1 and 5 on the scale; then tally your points in each section. At the end, you can add the totals from each section to calculate your total health assessment score.

You can find an interpretation of the results for each section and for your total health at the end of this chapter. If you discover anything of particular concern, I recommend that you consult your personal physician for additional help, guidance, and possibly treatment. I also suggest that you take the organizational health assessment in Appendix B to see if the same aspect or aspects of your organization's well-being need help, and can benefit from using the 4-Ps prescriptions presented in Part Two of this book.

## Personal Health Assessment

### *Person: Physical Health*

| 5 | 4 | 3 | 2 | 1 |
|---|---|---|---|---|
| Always | Often | Sometimes | Seldom | Never |

1. I am generally in good health without any major     5  4  3  2  1
   illnesses within the past five years.
2. I seek treatment immediately for any symptoms     5  4  3  2  1
   that occur, and take medication as prescribed.
3. I am a nonsmoker.     5  4  3  2  1
4. I consume less than two drinks of alcohol per day.  5  4  3  2  1
5. I maintain my ideal weight by eating a     5  4  3  2  1
   well-balanced diet and exercising at least three
   times a week.
6. I am free of cardiac risk factors such as high blood  5  4  3  2  1
   pressure, smoking, high cholesterol, or family
   history of heart disease.
7. I sleep for at least six hours a night and feel rested  5  4  3  2  1
   when I wake up.
8. My home and office are free of clutter.     5  4  3  2  1
9. I balance my checkbook regularly and have a     5  4  3  2  1
   regular savings plan.
10. I have adequate retirement savings.     5  4  3  2  1

### *Total Person: Physical Health Score Calculation*
Put the total number of responses for each point value on the left
and multiply by that point value.

   Then, add the totals.

$$\underline{\hspace{2cm}} \times 5 = \underline{\hspace{2cm}}$$

$$+ \underline{\hspace{2cm}} \times 4 = \underline{\hspace{2cm}}$$

$$+ \underline{\hspace{2cm}} \times 3 = \underline{\hspace{2cm}}$$

$$+ \underline{\hspace{2cm}} \times 2 = \underline{\hspace{2cm}}$$

$$+ \underline{\hspace{2cm}} \times 1 = \underline{\hspace{2cm}}$$

**Person: Physical Health Total =** \underline{\hspace{2cm}}

## Planning: Mental Health

| 5 | 4 | 3 | 2 | 1 |
|---|---|---|---|---|
| Always | Often | Sometimes | Seldom | Never |

1. I have a clear vision for my life.                     5  4  3  2  1
2. I have a strategic plan for my life.                   5  4  3  2  1
3. I update my life plan at regular intervals.            5  4  3  2  1
4. My memory is good.                                     5  4  3  2  1
5. I do mental exercises regularly.                       5  4  3  2  1
6. I am alert (rarely confused).                          5  4  3  2  1
7. I feel calm (rarely anxious).                          5  4  3  2  1
8. I have a positive attitude without                     5  4  3  2  1
   depressive thoughts.
9. I seek professional mental health                      5  4  3  2  1
   counseling, if needed.
10. I am free of chemical/stimulant addictions  5  4  3  2  1
    (alcohol/drugs/food/cigarettes/video
    games).

## Total Planning: Mental Health Score Calculation

Put the total number of responses for each point value on the left and multiply by that point value.

Then, add the totals.

$$\underline{\hspace{2cm}} \times 5 = \underline{\hspace{2cm}}$$
$$+\underline{\hspace{2cm}} \times 4 = \underline{\hspace{2cm}}$$
$$+\underline{\hspace{2cm}} \times 3 = \underline{\hspace{2cm}}$$
$$+\underline{\hspace{2cm}} \times 2 = \underline{\hspace{2cm}}$$
$$+\underline{\hspace{2cm}} \times 1 = \underline{\hspace{2cm}}$$

**Planning: Mental Health Total** = \underline{\hspace{2cm}}

## Passion: Emotional Health

| 5 | 4 | 3 | 2 | 1 |
|---|---|---|---|---|
| Always | Often | Sometimes | Seldom | Never |

1. I feel passion for my work.  5  4  3  1  1
2. I have a great deal of energy and do not  5  4  3  2  1
   feel stressed out.
3. I am optimistic.  5  4  3  2  1
4. I am even-tempered (rarely angry).  5  4  3  2  1
5. I am confident (rarely afraid).  5  4  3  2  1
6. I experience joy in my life.  5  4  3  2  1
7. I am able to recover from losses.  5  4  3  2  1
8. I can cope with adversity.  5  4  3  2  1
9. I am excited about my life.  5  4  3  2  1
10. I apologize or make amends if indicated.  5  4  3  2  1

## Total Passion: Emotional Health Score Calculation

Put the total number of responses for each point value on the left and multiply by that point value.

Then, add the totals.

$$\underline{\hspace{2cm}} \times 5 = \underline{\hspace{2cm}}$$

$$+ \underline{\hspace{2cm}} \times 4 = \underline{\hspace{2cm}}$$

$$+ \underline{\hspace{2cm}} \times 3 = \underline{\hspace{2cm}}$$

$$+ \underline{\hspace{2cm}} \times 2 = \underline{\hspace{2cm}}$$

$$+ \underline{\hspace{2cm}} \times 1 = \underline{\hspace{2cm}}$$

**Passion: Emotional Health Total** = \underline{\hspace{2cm}}

## Purpose: Spiritual Health

| 5 | 4 | 3 | 2 | 1 |
|---|---|---|---|---|
| Always | Often | Sometimes | Seldom | Never |

1. I feel a sense of purpose for my life.    5   4   3   2   1
2. I have and follow a personal mission statement.    5   4   3   2   1
3. I know and live in accordance with my core values.    5   4   3   2   1
4. I live my life with integrity, ensuring my actions match my words.    5   4   3   2   1
5. My life includes service to others.    5   4   3   2   1
6. I trust that the universe will bring me all that I need at the right time.    5   4   3   2   1
7. I experience unexpected occurrences that move my life forward.    5   4   3   2   1
8. I follow a daily spiritual practice.    5   4   3   2   1
9. I believe in some form of a higher power.    5   4   3   2   1
10. I pray and/or meditate regularly.    5   4   3   2   1

### Total Purpose: Spiritual Health Score Calculation

Put the total number of responses for each point value on the left and multiply by that point value.

Then, add the totals.

$$\underline{\hspace{2cm}} \times 5 = \underline{\hspace{2cm}}$$
$$+ \underline{\hspace{2cm}} \times 4 = \underline{\hspace{2cm}}$$
$$+ \underline{\hspace{2cm}} \times 3 = \underline{\hspace{2cm}}$$
$$+ \underline{\hspace{2cm}} \times 2 = \underline{\hspace{2cm}}$$
$$+ \underline{\hspace{2cm}} \times 1 = \underline{\hspace{2cm}}$$

**Purpose: Spiritual Health Total = \underline{\hspace{2cm}}**

## Total Health Assessment Score

Person: Physical Health   Total _____

+ Planning: Mental Health   Total _____

+ Passion: Emotional Health Total _____

+ Purpose: Spiritual Health   Total _____

**Total Health Assessment Score** = _____

## Interpretation of Scores

To assess your results, tally the scores in each section, and then read the following interpretations. You can calculate your total health assessment score by adding the scores from each section. Its interpretation is at the end of this chapter.

### *Person: Physical Health*

### 40–50 . . . Physically Fit

Congratulations! You are taking good care of yourself physically. All aspects of your physical health including your body, environment, and finances are in good shape. This good health enhances your leadership skills.

### 20–39 . . . Physically Neglected

You have not been paying as much attention to your physical health as you should, and may have some minor health problems that need appropriate treatment. You would probably also benefit from paying more attention to your environment and your finances, which may enhance your ability to do the same in your organization.

### Less than 20 . . . Physically Unhealthy

You have not been taking good care of yourself and need to pay more attention to your physical health and well-being. You probably do not follow a good diet and exercise regimen. You also may need to pay more attention to your personal and professional environments, and/or may have trouble keeping your finances in order. These physical difficulties are likely impacting your organization negatively.

## Planning: Mental Health

### 40–50 . . . Mentally Fit

Congratulations! Your mental state is healthy. There are no significant mental blocks or barriers that would limit your ability to create a wonderful life vision and strategic plan for yourself, and lead your organization to great heights.

### 20–39 . . . Mentally Challenged

There are some mental barriers you must overcome before you can create a new vision and plan for where you want to go in your life. You may need to seek professional counseling. The exercises in Chapter 7 can assist you with this planning process; however, complete them only after you have successfully removed any mental blocks that might keep you from leading successfully.

### Less than 20 . . . Mentally Overwhelmed

You presently have significant mental distress that is limiting your leadership ability. It would be best to seek professional help to remove any mental barriers that exist and begin a healing process that can restore you to a mentally healthy state.

## Passion: Emotional Health

### 40–50 . . . Emotionally Healthy

Congratulations! You are emotionally stable and well balanced, without any significant emotional blocks. You will be able to develop your life vision and strategic plan with ease, and your positive emotional outlook will enhance your ability to lead.

### 20–39 . . . Emotionally Distressed

You are currently undergoing a fair amount of emotional stress, and may lack a sense of passion in your life. You must identify what is blocking you emotionally before working on your life vision and strategic plan. You may find some of the methods presented in Chapter 6 helpful in doing so. Emotional clarity will help you find passion and purpose in your professional life as well.

## Less than 20 . . . Emotionally Blocked

You have some deep-seated emotional issues that you need to face before you can live a balanced life and be a highly effective leader. You may need professional help to overcome whatever is blocking you.

## Purpose: Spiritual Health

## 40–50 . . . Spiritually Connected

Congratulations! You have a strong sense of the spiritual in your daily life and feel the wonder and interconnectedness of the universe. You likely follow a regular spiritual practice and are living a life of integrity. You are in touch with your life purpose and core values, which are reflected in your daily work. You have a high ability to lead due to your solid spiritual foundation.

## 20–39 . . . Spiritually Searching

You have some sense that there is a higher power at work in the universe that connects us all, but your spiritual practice is inconsistent. You may need to connect with your inner being on a regular basis and make sure you are living your life on purpose and in accordance with your core values. You may also want to make sure that your core values are spiritually based. Once you accomplish this, your work life and ability to lead will benefit by being more on target and connected.

## Less than 20 . . . Spiritually Bankrupt

Your life lacks integrity and purpose. You feel disconnected from others and most likely from a higher power. You do not sense the wonder of the universe and are in need of connecting at a deeper level with your inner divine self. You lead your organization without a spiritual connection or without spiritually based values, which may cause you to lead it astray, choosing profits and growth at all costs.

## Total Health

### 160–200...Health in Excellent Balance

Congratulations! You are living a life that balances the physical, mental, emotional, and spiritual aspects of your personal health. There are few barriers to your creating a fulfilling and rewarding life, and you have the essential ingredients for being a highly effective leader.

### 120–159...Health in Good Balance

Although your health is in reasonably good balance, there may be some aspect or aspects that need further attention. The exercises in Part Two may be quite useful as you balance your personal health and build a healthy organization.

### 80–119...Health in Fair Balance

There are some significant areas of your health that need attention and that are limiting your leadership effectiveness. Some of the exercises in this book may help bring balance back into your life, but you may need to seek further professional counseling to remove blocks or barriers that may exist.

### Less than 80...Health Out of Balance

You are living a very unhealthy life at the present time. Things must change quickly if you are to live a balanced, fulfilling life and be an effective leader. You should seek the services of a physician or mental health professional to get back on track. Some of the prescriptions in Part Two may also be of benefit.

# APPENDIX B

# Organizational Health Assessment

This assessment tool is divided into four sections, reflecting the 4 Ps analogous to the four aspects of your personal health: People and Physical Assets, Planning, Passion, and Purpose. Each section contains ten questions with a five-point answer scale that ranges from 5 "Always" to 1 "Never." Please rate your organization between 1 and 5 on the scale; then go back and tally your scores for each section. You can calculate a total score for your organization's health by adding the scores from the four sections. You can ask your leadership team to do the same.

You will find an interpretation of results for each section at the end of the assessment, as well as one for your total organizational health score. If any of your organization's 4 Ps is out of balance, Part Two will provide methods to help you correct the situation in a timely manner. This transformation process will involve you, as well as many other people; you can conduct it using the format of the strategic transformation summit outlined in Chapter 10. It may also benefit you to seek professional guidance from an organizational development consultant or an executive coach as you lead your organization on a path of renewal and revitalization.

# Organizational Health Assessment

## People and Physical Assets

| 5 | 4 | 3 | 2 | 1 |
|---|---|---|---|---|
| Always | Often | Sometimes | Seldom | Never |

1. Our staff is healthy and rarely misses work due to poor health.    5  4  3  2  1
2. Our staff is dedicated, hardworking, and productive.    5  4  3  2  1
3. Our organization is fully staffed and has low turnover.    5  4  3  2  1
4. Our customers/membership numbers and revenues are growing.    5  4  3  2  1
5. Our organization encourages learning and growth.    5  4  3  2  1
6. Staff morale is high.    5  4  3  2  1
7. Our organization hits its financial targets and has adequate reserves.    5  4  3  2  1
8. Our organization's physical environment is conducive to maximizing productivity.    5  4  3  2  1
9. Our equipment is in good operating condition.    5  4  3  2  1
10. Our building is well maintained.    5  4  3  2  1

## Total People and Physical Assets Score Calculation

Write the total number of responses for each point value on the left and multiply by that point value.

    Then, add the totals.

$$\underline{\hspace{3cm}} \times 5 = \underline{\hspace{3cm}}$$
$$+ \underline{\hspace{3cm}} \times 4 = \underline{\hspace{3cm}}$$
$$+ \underline{\hspace{3cm}} \times 3 = \underline{\hspace{3cm}}$$
$$+ \underline{\hspace{3cm}} \times 2 = \underline{\hspace{3cm}}$$
$$+ \underline{\hspace{3cm}} \times 1 = \underline{\hspace{3cm}}$$

**People and Physical Assets Total** = \underline{\hspace{3cm}}

# Planning

| 5 | 4 | 3 | 2 | 1 |
|---|---|---|---|---|
| Always | Often | Sometimes | Seldom | Never |

1. Our organization has a compelling vision statement.     5 4 3 2 1
2. Our organization follows an annual or biannual strategic planning process.     5 4 3 2 1
3. Our goals and objectives are doable with adequate resources.     5 4 3 2 1
4. We communicate our goals and objectives throughout the organization.     5 4 3 2 1
5. We enjoy an easy exchange of ideas.     5 4 3 2 1
6. We value vision, creativity, and innovation.     5 4 3 2 1
7. New ideas surface easily in our organization.     5 4 3 2 1
8. We value thinking time.     5 4 3 2 1
9. We use win-win strategies in our negotiations.     5 4 3 2 1
10. Our organization gives "mental health days" as a benefit to relieve stress.     5 4 3 2 1

## Total Planning Score Calculation

Write the total number of responses for each point value on the left and multiply by that point value.

Then add the totals.

$$\underline{\hspace{2cm}} \times 5 = \underline{\hspace{2cm}}$$
$$+ \underline{\hspace{2cm}} \times 4 = \underline{\hspace{2cm}}$$
$$+ \underline{\hspace{2cm}} \times 3 = \underline{\hspace{2cm}}$$
$$+ \underline{\hspace{2cm}} \times 2 = \underline{\hspace{2cm}}$$
$$+ \underline{\hspace{2cm}} \times 1 = \underline{\hspace{2cm}}$$

**Planning Total** = _____

## Passion

| 5 | 4 | 3 | 2 | 1 |
|---|---|---|---|---|
| Always | Often | Sometimes | Seldom | Never |

1. Our organization's culture empowers individuals.          5  4  3  2  1
2. Our staff is enthusiastic about their work.          5  4  3  2  1
3. The organization is free of internal warring fiefdoms.          5  4  3  1  1
4. We value emotional intelligence and promote leaders who exhibit it.          5  4  3  2  1
5. We have an open environment that supports growth and creativity.          5  4  3  2  1
6. We have a very collaborative culture.          5  4  3  2  1
7. We utilize effective conflict resolution methods that use win-win strategies.          5  4  3  2  1
8. We do not tolerate people with volatile tempers.          5  4  3  2  1
9. People do not feel intimidated in our organization.          5  4  3  2  1
10. We encourage in-person communication.          5  4  3  2  1

## Total Passion Score Calculation

Write the total number of responses for each point value on the left and multiply by that point value.

   Then, add the totals.

$$\underline{\hspace{3cm}} \times 5 = \underline{\hspace{3cm}}$$
$$+\underline{\hspace{3cm}} \times 4 = \underline{\hspace{3cm}}$$
$$+\underline{\hspace{3cm}} \times 3 = \underline{\hspace{3cm}}$$
$$+\underline{\hspace{3cm}} \times 2 = \underline{\hspace{3cm}}$$
$$+\underline{\hspace{3cm}} \times 1 = \underline{\hspace{3cm}}$$

**Passion Total** = \underline{\hspace{3cm}}

## Purpose

| 5 | 4 | 3 | 2 | 1 |
|---|---|---|---|---|
| Always | Often | Sometimes | Seldom | Never |

1. Our organization's mission statement is relevant in today's marketplace.    5 4 3 2 1
2. Our organization is in sync with its mission.    5 4 3 2 1
3. We clearly communicate our organization's mission/ purpose and make sure that people at all levels in the organization understand it.    5 4 3 2 1
4. We widely communicate and adhere to our core values.    5 4 3 2 1
5. Our organization always acts with a high level of integrity (what we say is what we do).    5 4 3 2 1
6. Our organization is internally consistent with its core values.    5 4 3 2 1
7. Our organization uses corporate retreats or summits as part of our renewal process.    5 4 3 2 1
8. We value the inner dimension in the creative process.    5 4 3 2 1
9. Unexpected occurrences often help move our organization forward.    5 4 3 2 1
10. Our values reflect service to others.    5 4 3 2 1

## Total Purpose Score Calculation

Write the total number of responses for each point value on the left and multiply by that point value.

Then, add the totals.

$$\underline{\hspace{2cm}} \times 5 = \underline{\hspace{2cm}}$$
$$+ \underline{\hspace{2cm}} \times 4 = \underline{\hspace{2cm}}$$
$$+ \underline{\hspace{2cm}} \times 3 = \underline{\hspace{2cm}}$$
$$+ \underline{\hspace{2cm}} \times 2 = \underline{\hspace{2cm}}$$
$$+ \underline{\hspace{2cm}} \times 1 = \underline{\hspace{2cm}}$$
$$\textbf{Purpose Total} = \underline{\hspace{2cm}}$$

# Total Organizational Health Assessment Score

People and Physical Assets Total _____

+ Planning                    Total _____

+ Passion                     Total _____

+ Purpose                     Total _____

**Total Organizational Health Assessment Score =** _____

# Interpretation of Scores

To interpret your overall results, tally each section's score and read the following interpretations. Then tally your Total Organizational Health Assessment Score by adding the scores from each section, and read the interpretation at the end of this section.

## People and Physical Assets

### 40–50... Physically Fit Organization
Congratulations! Your organization is in excellent physical shape. Its finances are in order, and it is prospering. Your staff is healthy and productive, and your physical environment is in good condition. Your organization is thriving. You want to make sure that you maintain an ongoing renewal process to ensure that this continues.

### 20–39... Physically Deteriorating Organization
You may need to pay more attention to your organization's physical condition. Your staff may not be healthy. Your equipment and space might need repair or replacement, and your finances and customer base may be decreasing. Take some time to correct these deficiencies.

### Less than 20... Physically Deficient Organization
Your organization is in decline and needs your prompt attention. Your staff and the environment in which they work are not healthy.

Equipment is probably in need of repair or replacement. You have financial troubles. Physical improvements will help to create a healthy environment in your workplace.

## *Planning*

### 40–50...Mentally Fit Organization

Congratulations! Your organization allows new ideas to flourish. You have a compelling organizational vision and strategic plan, and you reward creativity and innovation. Your organization also values a positive attitude, and probably gives time off to relieve mental stress.

### 20–39...Mentally Challenged Organization

You place limitations on creative and intellectual ideas at your organization. Because of these mental blocks, your ability to create a new vision and your strategic planning process may be impaired. It is advisable to remove these barriers before moving forward to create a compelling vision and plan of action.

### Less than 20...Mentally Overwhelmed Organization

Your organization has significant mental blocks that limit its ability to develop new ideas and strategic new directions. In order to develop your organization to its full potential, you must remove these blocks before continuing the visioning and planning processes.

## *Passion*

### 40–50...Emotionally Healthy Organization

Congratulations! Your organization values emotional intelligence and works to minimize emotional tension in the workplace. There is a positive esprit de corps and high staff morale. Your culture is most likely collaborative, with effective conflict resolution mechanisms in place. Your leadership skills are reflected in the positive communications that take place throughout your organization.

## 20–39 . . . Emotionally Distressed Organization

Your organization's productivity is somewhat limited due to emotional tensions that exist, and you may be tolerating warring fiefdoms or tyrannical managers. Staff morale is likely down because some leaders fail to tune into their employees. There may be underlying barriers that prevent clear communication. Holding regular check-in sessions with management staff and key employees could help ferret out communication problems and resolve underlying issues.

## Less than 20 . . . Emotionally Blocked Organization

Your organization is emotionally blocked, with serious tensions that you need to remove or overcome in order to prosper. You need to lead by example so others can see that positive change is possible.

### *Purpose*

## 40–50 . . . Purposeful (Spiritually Sound)

Congratulations! Your organization has a strong sense of purpose that is in sync with the marketplace. Its mission and core values include service to others and are clearly communicated throughout. Its integrity is high, and you have a well-respected corporate identity.

## 20–39 . . . Drifting Off Purpose (Spiritually Ungrounded)

Your organization is not well grounded, and you lack a strong sense of purpose. Its mission and core values may not be in sync with the current marketplace, or they may be based on false assumptions. Your organization may lack integrity, and erroneous beliefs and misleading values may take precedence.

## Less than 20 . . . Purpose Out of Alignment (Spiritually Bankrupt)

Your organization has lost its way. Its mission and purpose may have become irrelevant over time. Your employees likely don't adhere to core values, thus tarnishing your corporate identity. In essence, your ladder to success is leaning against the wrong wall. The future of your organization is not bright, unless you make significant changes.

## Total Organizational Health

### 160–200 . . . Healthy Organization

Congratulations! Your organization is in good shape, physically, mentally, emotionally, and spiritually, and the 4 Ps—People and Physical Assets, Planning, Passion, and Purpose—are functioning very well. It is important for your organization to have a renewal process in place to assure long-lasting health.

### 120–159 . . . Ailing Organization

Your organization's health is starting to show signs and symptoms of poor health. There may be one or two of the 4 Ps that would benefit from additional attention and focus. The recommendations and processes in Part Two of this book will likely help quite a bit in restoring your organization's health and maximizing its long-lasting success.

### 80–119 . . . Poor Health Organization

Some aspects of your organization's health need prompt attention. The healing process can begin under your leadership by referring to Part Two. Many workable solutions are available to help you achieve lasting success.

### Less than 80 . . . Critically Ill Organization

Your organization is unhealthy and in immediate need of resuscitation. The prescriptions at the end of each chapter in Part Two will help you get your organization off life support. The strategic transformation summit outlined in Chapter 10 may be helpful in getting key leaders involved in the healing and renewal process, which is necessary to get back on track.

# NOTES

## Chapter 1  Introducing the 4-Ps Model for Strategic Transformation

1. Roger Collier, "American Medical Association Membership Woes Continue," *Canadian Medical Association Journal* 183, no. 11 (2011): doi: 10.153/cmaj.109–3943.
2. Roger Collier, "American Medical Association Membership Woes Continue," *Canadian Medical Association Journal* 183, no. 11 (2011): doi: 10.153/cmaj.109–3943.
3. Lev Grossman and Harry McCracken, "The Inventor of the Future," *Time*, October 17, 2011, http://www.time.com/time/magazine/article/0,9171,2096294,00.html.
4. Scott DeCarlo, "The World's 25 Most Valuable Companies: Apple Is Now On Top," *Forbes*, "Running the Numbers" blog, http://www.forbes.com/sites/scottdecarlo/2011/08/11/the-worlds-25-most-valuable-companies-apple-is-now-on-top/.

## Chapter 2  The 4 Ps and Effective Leadership: Assessing Your Leadership Style

1. Scott DeCarlo, "The World's 25 Most Valuable Companies: Apple Is Now On Top," *Forbes*, "Running the Numbers" blog, http://www.forbes.com/sites/scottdecarlo/2011/08/11/the-worlds-25-most-valuable-companies-apple-is-now-on-top/.

2. John W. Gardner, *On Leadership* (New York: Free Press, 1993), 48–49.
3. F. Hesselbein, M. Goldsmith, and R. Beckhard, *The Leader of the Future: New Visions, Strategies and Practices for the Next Era* (New Jersey: Jossey-Bass, 1997): 193.
4. R. M. Yerkes, and J. D. Dodson, "The Relation of Strength of Stimulus to Rapidity of Habit-Formation," *Journal of Comparative Neurology and Psychology* 18, (1908): 459-482.
5. D. Goleman, R. E. Boyatzis, and A. McKee, *Primal Leadership: Learning to Lead with Emotional Intelligence* (Boston: Harvard Business Review Press, 2004): 26.
6. R. K. Greenleaf, L. C. Spears, and S. R. Covey, *Servant Leadership: A Journey into the Nature of Legitimate Power and Greatness 25th Anniversary Edition* (New York: Paulist Press, 2002).
7. Joseph Jaworski, *Synchronicity: The Inner Path of Leadership* (San Francisco: Berrett-Koehler Publishers, 1996): 119.
8. Stephen R. Covey, *The 7 Habits of Highly Effective People* (New York: Free Press, 1989).
9. John W. Gardner, *On Leadership* (New York: Free Press, 1993): 121.

# Chapter 3   The 4 Ps and Organizational Transformation: Assessing Your Organization

1. S. Keller and C. Price, *Beyond Performance: How Great Organizations Build Ultimate Competitive Advantage* (New York: John Wiley & Sons, 2011): 31-33.
2. F. Hesselbein, M. Goldsmith, and R. Beckhard, *The Leader of the Future: New Visions, Strategies and Practices for the Next Era* (New Jersey: Jossey-Bass, 1997): 275.
3. D. Goleman, A. McKee, and R. E. Boyatzis, *Primal Leadership: Realizing the Power of Emotional Intelligence* (Boston: Harvard Business Review Press, 2002): 4.

4. S. R. Covey, A. R. Merrill, and R. R. Merrill, *First Things First: To Live, to Love, to Leave a Legacy* (New York: Simon and Schuster, 1994): 220-221.

5. D. Goleman, A. McKee, and R. E. Boyatzis, *Primal Leadership: Realizing the Power of Emotional Intelligence* (Boston: Harvard Business Review Press, 2002): 17-18.

6. S. Lyubomirsky, L. King, and E. Diener, "The Benefits of Frequent Positive Affect: Does Happiness Lead to Success?" *Psychological Bulletin* 131 (2005): 803-855.

7. S. Keller and C. Price, *Beyond Performance: How Great Organizations Build Ultimate Competitive Advantage* (New York: John Wiley & Sons, 2011): 32.

8. S. Keller and C. Price, *Beyond Performance: How Great Organizations Build Ultimate Competitive Advantage* (New York: John Wiley & Sons, 2011).

# Chapter 4   The Treatment from Inside Out: Transforming Your Organization

1. Wendy Kaufman, "Netflix Stock Down 75 Percent From Its July Peak," *NPR Business*, October 26, 2011, http://www.npr.org/2011/10/26/141734200/netflix-stock-down-75-percent-from-its-july-peak.

2. Reed Hastings, "An Explanation and Some Reflections," *Netflix US & Canada Blog*, http://blog.netflix.com/2011/09/explanation-and-some-reflections.html.

3. Gary Friedman, "TV streaming is new star for Netflix," *Los Angeles Times*, February 5, 2012, sec. B.

4. Rosabeth Moss Kanter, "How Great Companies Think Differently," *Harvard Business Review*, November 2011, 66-78.

5. Google Finance, http://www.google.com/finance.

6. "About," Zappos.com, http://about.zappos.com/our-unique-culture/zappos-core-values.

7. Tony Hsieh, interviewed by Barbara Walters, *20/20*, ABC News, October 28, 2011.

## Chapter 5   Restoring Passion in the Workplace

1. Daniel Goleman, *Emotional Intelligence: Why It Can Matter More Than IQ* (New York: Bantam Books, 1995).
2. Norman V. Peale, *The Power of Positive Thinking*, (New York: Simon & Schuster, 1952).
3. Wade Boggs, quoted in *American Athlete Quotes*, Successories, http://www.successories.com/iquote/category/121/american-athlete-quotes/254.
4. Rich Maloof, "Monday Morning Heart Attacks . . . and Other Health Risks by the Day of the Week," MSN *Health & Fitness*, February 24, 2011.
5. L. Trivieri and J. W. Anderson, *Alternative Medicine: The Definitive Guide* (New York: Random House, 2002).
6. Shawn Achor, "Positive Intelligence," *Harvard Business Review*, January/February 2012, 100-102.
7. Candace B. Pert, *Molecules of Emotion*, (New York: Touchstone, 1999).
8. Rhonda Byrne, *The Secret* (New York: Atria Books, 2006).
9. L. Little, and B. McGuire, "U.S. Employers Added No New Jobs In August," ABC World News Money, September 2, 2011, http://abcnews.go.com/Business/unemployment-rate-unchanged-91-percent-jobs-added-august/story?id=14429363#.T5NIpphOEUU.
10. Dale Carnegie, *How to Win Friends and Influence People* (New York: Simon & Schuster, 1981).
11. John P. Kotter, *Leading Change* (Boston: Harvard Business Review Press, 1996).
12. William Bridges, *Transitions: Making Sense of Life's Changes* (Cambridge: Da Capo Press, 2004).

13. "Major Depressive Disorder Among Adults," National Institute of Mental Health, http://www.nimh.nih.gov/statistics/1MDD_ ADULT.shtml.
14. P. E. Greenberg, R. C. Kessler, H. G. Birnbaum, S. A. Leong, S. W. Lowe, P. A. Berglund, and P. K. Corey-Lisle, "The Economic Burden of Depression in the United States: How Did It Change Between 1990 and 2000?," *The Journal of Clinical Psychology*, 64, no. 12 (2003): 1465-1475.
15. Norman Cousins, *Anatomy of an Illness as Perceived by the Patient* (New York: Batam Books, 1991).
16. Norine Dworkin-McDaniel, "Touching Makes You Healthier," CNN Health, January 5, 2011, http://www.cnn.com/2011/ HEALTH/01/05/touching.makes.you.healthier.health/index .html.
17. D. Goleman, A. McKee, and R. E. Boyatzis, *Primal Leadership: Realizing the Power of Emotional Intelligence* (Boston: Harvard Business Review Press, 2002).

## Chapter 6    Creating and Communicating a Compelling Organizational Vision

1. M. Co, H. Foo, and A. Palmer, "UCLA Success Factors Study," Anderson School of Management, (1997).
2. *Einstein's Big Idea*, directed by Gary Johnstone (2005; Arlington, VA: Public Broadcasting Service, 2005), DVD.
3. Irwin Press, *Patient Satisfaction: Defining, Measuring, and Improving the Experience of Care* (Chicago: Health Administration Press, 2002).
4. Stephen R. Covey, *The 7 Habits of Highly Effective People* (Whitby: Fireside Publishing, 1990): 235.
5. W. Bennis, and J. Goldsmith, *Learning to Lead: A Workbook on Becoming a Leader* (Boston: Addison-Wesley, 1997): 116.
6. M. Argyle, V. Salter, H. Nicholson, M. Williams, and P. Burgess, "The Communication of Inferior and Superior Attitudes by

Verbal and Nonverbal Signals," *British Journal of Social and Clinical Psychology* 9, no. 3 (1970): 222-231.

7. Debbie Sanders, "What Is It Worth: The Business Case for Communicating the Value of Total Rewards," *Horizon* (2001).

8. John P. Kotter, *Leading Change* (Boston: Harvard Business Review Press, 1996): 90.

## Chapter 7 Developing a Strategic Plan for Organizational Transformation

1. George T. Doran, "There's a S.M.A.R.T. Way to Write Management's Goals and Objectives," *Management Review* 70, no. 11 (1981): 35-36.

2. Mark H. McCormack, *What They Don't Teach You at Harvard Business School: Notes from a Street-Smart Executive* (New York: Bantam Books, 1986).

3. Stephen R. Covey, *The 7 Habits of Highly Effective People* (New York: Free Press, 1989).

4. Jim Collins, *Good to Great: Why Some Companies Make the Leap . . . and Others Don't* (New York: Harper Business, 2001): 41.

5. Deepak Chopra, *The Seven Spiritual Laws of Success: A Practical Guide to the Fulfillment of Your Dreams* (San Rafael: Amber-Allen Publishing, 1994): 79-80.

## Chapter 8 Developing People, Transforming Your Culture

1. Tony Hsieh, interviewed by Barbara Walters, *20/20*, ABC News, October 28, 2011.

2. J. M. Citrin, and D. Ogden, "Succeeding at Succession," *Harvard Business Review*, November 2010, 1-4.

3. John C. Abell, "Aug. 6, 1997: Apple Rescued—by Microsoft," *Wired*, "This Day in Tech" blog, http://www.wired.com/thisdayintech/2009/08/dayintech_0806/.

4. Google Finance, http://www.google.com/finance.
5. Richard Barton, "Customer Service in the Public Sector," Asian Productivity Organization, http://www.apo-tokyo.org/productivity/055_prod.htm.
6. J. McGovern, M. Lindemann, M. Vergara, S. Murphy, L. Barker, and R. Warrenfeltz, "Maximizing the Impact of Executive Coaching: Behavioral Change, Organizational Outcomes, and Return on Investment," *The Manchester Review* 6, no. 1 (2001): 1-9.
7. Chip R. Bell, *Managers as Mentors 2 Ed: Building Partnerships for Learning* (San Francisco: Berrett-Koehler Publishers, 2002).
8. John P. Kotter, *Leading Change* (Boston: Harvard Business Review Press, 1996).
9. J. M. Corrigan, M. S. Donaldson, L. T. Kohn, T. McKay, and K. C. Pike, "To Err is Human: Building a Safer Health System," *Institute of Medicine*, (1999).

# Chapter 9   Making Success Last: The 5th P, Perseverance

1. David H. Donald, *Lincoln* (New York: Simon and Schuster, 1996).
2. David Brooks, "The C.E.O. in Politics," *New York Times*, January 12, 2012, http://www.nytimes.com/2012/01/13/opinion/brooks-the-ceo-in-politics.html.
3. W. Bennis, and J. Goldsmith, *Learning to Lead: A Workbook on Becoming a Leader* (New York: Basic Books, 2003).
4. J. Collins, and M. T. Hansen, *Great by Choice: Uncertainty, Chaso, and Luck—Why some Thrive Despite Them All* (New York: Harper Business, 2011).
5. K. Webley, "Top 10 Commonly Broken New Year's Resolutions," January, 1, 2012, http://www.time.com/time/specials/packages/article/0,28804,2040218_2040220_2040221,00.html.
6. John W. Gardner, *On Leadership* (New York: Free Press, 1993): 122.

7. Walter Isaacson, *Steve Jobs* (New York: Simon and Schuster, 2011).

8. Nick Bilton, "One on One: Walter Isaacson, Biographer of Steve Jobs," *Bits (Blog)*, http://bits.blogs.nytimes.com/2011/11/18/one-on-one-walter-isaacson-biographer-of-steve-jobs/.

9. Walter Isaacson, *Steve Jobs* (New York: Simon and Schuster, 2011).

10. J. Canfield, M. V. Hansen, and L. Hewitt, *The Power of Focus: How to Hit Your Business, Personal, and Financial Targets with Absolute Certainty* (Deerfield Beach: HCI, 2000).

## Chapter 10　The Final Prescription: A Strategic Transformation Summit

1. Jim Collins, *Good to Great: Why Some Companies Make the Leap . . . and Others Don't* (New York: Harper Business, 2001): 41.

# ABOUT THE AUTHOR

Dr. Susan Reynolds is the President and CEO of The Institute for Medical Leadership®, which for over 12 years has been conducting organizational assessments, leadership development seminars, executive and physician coaching, and strategic-planning retreats for numerous healthcare organizations, academic medical centers, business schools, and national and state medical associations.

A former emergency physician, emergency medical center CEO, and White House healthcare advisor, Dr. Reynolds is the creator and Program Director for the highly acclaimed Chief of Staff Boot Camp® program for hospital medical staff leaders. During the past nine years, nearly 2,000 physician leaders and healthcare executives have been trained through this program.

In 1993, Dr. Reynolds was appointed to the White House Health Professionals Review Group, serving as one of its few practicing physician members. She founded and led the Physician Executive Practices at both Heidrick & Struggles and Russell Reynolds Associates, two leading international executive search firms. She also founded the Malibu Emergency Room, served as the facility's CEO and chief physician for 12 years, and organized a tax-exempt charity that produced celebrity events to support emergency medical care in Malibu, California.

Dr. Reynolds currently serves on the Board of the Los Angeles County Medical Association and is a Delegate to the California Medical Association House of Delegates. In the past Dr. Reynolds has served as national Chair of Health Policy for the American

College of Emergency Physicians, President of the American Association of Women Emergency Physicians, Regional Governor of the American Medical Women's Association, and President of the Malibu Chamber of Commerce.

Dr. Reynolds is the recipient of numerous honors and recognitions including Woman of the Year, California's 44th Assembly District; *Malibu Times* Citizen of the Year, Los Angeles County Distinguished Service Award, and the American Medical Women's Association Community Service Award.

Dr. Reynolds received her A.B. with top honors from Vassar College, then obtained a Ph.D. in Biological Chemistry and an M.D. degree from UCLA. She completed a residency in internal medicine and a fellowship in cardiology, critical care medicine, and administrative medicine at UCLA and became a Diplomate of the American Board of Internal Medicine.

In her free time, Dr. Reynolds enjoys tennis, music, water sports, and time with her family, friends, and golden retriever.

# INDEX

## A

Active listening, 92–93
Affordable Care Act, "Obamacare," 20, 106
AMA. *See* American Medical Association (AMA)
American Leadership Forum, 32
American Medical Association (AMA), 19–23, 113, 143
Amundsen, Roald, 144, 147
*Anatomy of an Illness (Cousins)*, 74
Anger, resolving, 68–69
Apple, 23–24, 28, 124–125, 151
Attitude, effect of, 62–64
Attraction, Law of, 66
Audience, communicating with, 90–91
Auditory communicators, 98–101

## B

Bandler, Richard, 96
Barnes & Noble, 54
Bear Stearns, 16, 51
Bell, Chip, 131
Bennis, Warren, 143
Berkshire Hathaway, Code of Business Conduct and Ethics, 51–52
"Billionaire Secrets," 52
*The Blind Side* (movie), 132
Borders, 54
Boredom, dealing with, 66–68
Brainstorming, 109, 118, 119
Bresler, David, 82, 83, 85
Bridges, William, 70
Brooks, David, 143
Budget Rent-a-Car Corporation, 36
Buffett, Warren, 52
"Building Dynamic Organization," 17
Building *vs.* maintaining, 149–150
Burnout, recognizing, 72

## C

California Medical Association (CMA), 22, 125, 143, 169–172

California Medical Association's Annual Leadership Academy, 92
*Candid Camera*, 74
Canfield, Jack, 154
Carey, Drew, 73
Caring, power of, 75
Carnegie, Dale, 69
Central nervous system (CNS), information-processing systems in, 83
Chopra, Deepak, 117
Citrin, James, 124
CMA. *See* California Medical Association (CMA)
Coaching, 75, 127–130
Collins, Jim, 115, 144
Commitment, 145–146, 153–154
Communication, 69, 93–94, 133
Complaints, looking beyond, 38–40
Corcoran, Dustin, 169–172
Core values
    about, 50–51
    in 5Ps summit, 161–162
    as guideposts for success, 52–53
    purpose and, 58–59
    of Wall Street financial services firms, 51–52
Cousins, Norman, 74
Covey, Stephen, 33, 37, 55, 91, 109, 148
Creative Inner Advisor,® 85, 86, 87, 88
Creativity, happy employees and, 38
Cultural change, 135–136

## D

Developing people and transforming culture
    building effective teams, 132–134
    coaching to improve performance, 127–130
    investing in people, 135–136
    mentoring Generation Y, 130–132
    motivating others, 126–127
    physical assets, 137–139
    power of rewards, 136–137
    prescription for, 139–140
    value of right human capital, 124–125

Diagnostic tools, organizational assessment and, 17
Donald, David Herbert, 142
Drucker Foundation, 29, 36

E
Einstein, Albert, 85
Emotional aspect
    of an organization, 15
    mental aspect of leader's health and, 31
    of organizational health, 36
    of personal health, 29
Emotional Intelligence (Goleman), 31, 62
Emotional intelligence skills, 37
Emotions. See also Negative emotions
    biochemistry of, 65–66
    positive, power of, 63, 72–74
Endurance, 145, 147, 154–155
Environmental scan
    marketplace trends and, 80, 102
    in pre-summit preparation, 159–160
    strategic goals and, 106
Ernst & Young, 118

F
Fear, dispelling, 69–72
Feedback Loop, 119, 122, 167–168
Finances, organizations and, 138–139
Financial audit, 39
First Things First (Covey), 37
5Ps summit
    overview of the process, 161
    passion in, 162–163
    people and physical assets in, 165, 167
    planning in, 163–164
    purpose and core values in, 161–162
    time in, 165
Focus, 145, 146–147, 154, 167
4Ps and effective leadership. See Leadership style assessment

G
Ganey, Press, 89
Gardner, John, 29, 33, 148
Generation Y, mentoring, 130–132
Goal(s)
    developing objectives for, 110
    organizational, developing, 109–110
    prioritizing, 116–117, 122, 167
    setting, 107–108, 164–165
    telling others about, 118
    working backwards to set, 112
Goldsmith, Joan, 143

Goleman, Daniel, 31, 37, 38, 62, 75
Good to Great (Collins), 115, 159
Gordian-knot type, 87
Great by Choice (Collins), 144
Greenleaf, Robert, 32
Grinder, John, 96
Guided Imagery Exercise, 86–89, 102

H
Hansen, Mark Victor, 154
Harvard Business Review, 50, 64
Hastings, Reed, 49
Health, 29–34, 40–41, 66, 183
Healthcare industry, 56–59, 135
Healthy organization, 35–36, 37, 40
Heidrick & Struggles, 67, 82, 92, 95, 118, 124
Hewitt, Lee, 154
"How Great Companies Think Differently," 50
How to Win Friends and Influence People (Carnegie), 69
Hsieh, Tony, 52, 53, 124
Human capital, value of, 124–125

I
Institute for Medical Leadership,® 56, 143, 145
Internal alignment, healthy organization and, 40
The Inventure Group in Minneapolis, 30
Investing, in people, 135–136, 171
Isaacson, Walter, 152

J
Jaworski, Joseph, 32
Jobs, Steve, 24, 28
    as Interim CEO, 124–125
    passing of, 23
    perseverance of, 150–152
    vision of, 53–54
The Joint Commission (TJC), 31, 40, 137

K
Kanter, Rosabeth Moss, 50
Keller, Scott, 40
Kinesthic communicators, 98–101
King, Reverend Martin Luther, Jr., 80, 90
Kotter, John, 69, 102, 134

L
LACMA. See Los Angeles County Medical Association (LACMA)

Laughter, healing effect of, 74
Laurie, Hugh, 37
*The Leader of the Future* (Druker Foundation), 29, 36–37
Leaders. *See also* Leadership
    connecting with the audience, 90
    as motivators, 62
    negative feelings and, 64
    passion in the workplace and, 75–78
    personal strategic plan and, 120–121, 122
Leadership. *See also* Leadership style assessment
    organizational success and, 159
    of Steve Jobs, 24
    style of, 75
Leadership style assessment
    aspects of personal health, 28–29
    leadership and health, 29–34
    organization's health, 27–28
*Leading Change* (Kotter), 69, 102, 134
Lean or Six Sigma techniques, 39
*Learning to Lead* (Bennis and Goldsmith), 91, 143
Left-brain thinking, 83, 84, 89
Lehman Brothers, 16, 51
Leider, Richard J., 30
Licwinko, Mary Lou, 48
*Lincoln* (Donald), 142
Listening, 91–94
Los Angeles County Medical Association (LACMA), 56, 125
Loss, as phase 1 of transition, 70–71
Lucas, George, 151

**M**
*Managers as Mentors* (Bell), 131
Market analysis, 106, 121
Market assessment, 53–55
Marketplace trends, 106, 121
*Marx Brothers* (movie), 74
Massachusetts Medical Society, 47, 126
Matching and mirroring, 94–95, 96
McCain, John, 98
Mediators, resolving conflict and, 69
Mental aspect
    of an organization, 15
    emotional aspect of leader's health and, 31
    of health, 29
    of organizational health, 36
Mentoring Generation Y, 130–132
Meriter Medical Group (MMG), 101–103, 107
Merrill Lynch, 51
Mission statement
    of Barnes & Noble, 54
    of Borders, 54–55

of California Medical Association, 170
of Heidrick & Struggles, 67
of Institute for Medical Leadership,® 56
of Lehman Brothers, 51
of Massachusetts Medical Society, 47
of Netflix, 49
personal, 55–56
review of, 50
San Francisco Medical Society, 47–48
of Zappos, 52–53
MMG. *See* Meriter Medical Group (MMG)
*Molecules of Emotion* (Pert), 65
Motivation, 31, 126–127

**N**
National Institute of Mental Health (NIMH), 65, 70
Negative emotions
    dealing with boredom, 66–68
    dispelling fear, 69–72
    effect of, 62–65
    resolving anger, 68–69
Netflix Story, 48–49
Neuro-Linguistic Programming (NLP), 96–101
Neutral zone. *See* Void
New beginning, as phase 3 in transition, 71–72
*New York Times*, 143
NeXT Computing, 151
NIMH. *See* National Institute of Mental Health (NIMH)
NLP. *See* Neuro-Linguistic Programming (NLP)
Northeast Georgia Health System, 135

**O**
Obama, Barack, 97, 98
Obamacare. *See* Affordable Care Act, "Obamacare"
Objectives, 110, 112, 116–117, 122
Ogden, Dayton, 124
*On Leadership* (Gardner), 29
Opportunities, open to, 117–118, 122
Organizational analysis, internal and external, 106
Organizational assessment. *See also* Organizational health assessment
    4Ps and effective leadership, 27–34
    4Ps and organizational transformation, 35–41
    4-Ps Model for Strategic Transformation, 13–26
    tools, 39

Organizational health assessment
    interpretation of scores, 190–193
    passion, 188, 191–192
    people and physical assets, 186–187,
        190–191
    planning, 187, 191
    in pre-summit preparation, 160–161
    purpose, 189, 190, 192–193
Organizational integrity, 16
Organizational purpose and core values
    realignment
    core values, 50–53
    healthcare industry changes, 56–59
    market assessment, 53–55
    mission statement, 46–48
    personal mission statements, 55–56
Organizational structure, core values and, 50
Organizational success
    of Apple, 23–24
    choice of leadership and, 159
    core values as guideposts for, 52–53
    creating, 41
    4Ps of organizational transformation and, 16
    sense of passion and, 62
Organizational transformation
    creating and communicating organizational
        vision, 79–103
    developing people and transforming culture,
        123–140
    developing strategic plan for organizational
        transformation, 105–122
    4Ps and, 14–16, 35–41
    organization's purpose and core values
        realignment, 46–59
    perseverance and, 141–156
    restoring passion in workplace, 61–78
    strategic transformation summit, 157–173
Organization(s). See also Mission statement;
    Organizational assessment; Organizational
    purpose and core values realignment;
    Organizational success; Organizational
    transformation; Vision
    building dynamic, 17
    diagnosing form outside-in, 17–18
    looking within, 19–20
Organization's human capital. See People


P
PACE® Color Palette, 132–133
Pacesetting, as leadership style, 75
Palin, Sarah, 97
Passion
    American Medical Association and, 20,
        21–22
    as an aspect of mental health, 29
    of Apple employees and customers, 24
    as emotional aspect of organizational health,
        36
    emotional health score, 178, 181–182
    in 5Ps summit, 162–163
    in healthy organization, 37
    as motivator, 127
    organizational health assessment and, 188,
        191–192
    in 4Ps Model of Strategic Transformation,
        14, 17
    vision and, 90
    in workplace, 61–78
Patient Satisfaction (Ganey), 89
Patient satisfaction, in Emergency Department,
    89–90
Peale, Norman Vincent, 63
People, 34, 39. See also Developing people and
    transforming culture
    American Medical Association and, 19, 22
    in 5Ps summit, 165, 167
    organizational health assessment and, 186,
        190
    as physical aspect of organizational health,
        36
    in 4Ps Model of Strategic Transformation,
        14, 17
    talented, Apple and, 24
Performance, 31, 40–41, 127–130
Perseverance
    Apple and, 24
    assessing, 152–153
    building vs. maintaining, 149–150
    in business, 150–152
    California Medical Association and, 171
    creating lasting success and, 41
    elements of, 145–149
    in 5Ps summit, 167–169
    of individuals and organizations, 34
    prescription for, 156
    success and, 16
    time frame challenge, 150
Person, 29, 176, 180–181
Personal health, aspects of, 28–29
Personal health assessment, 175–183
Personal mission statements, 55–56
Personal strategic planning, 120–121
Pert, Candice, 65–66
Physical aspect
    of an organization, 14
    of an organization's health, 36
    of personal health, 28–29
Physical assets, 137–140, 165, 167, 186, 190
Physicians Plus Insurance Corporation (P-Plus,
    for short), 101
Pixar Animation Studios, 151

Plamondon, William, 36–37
Planning
    American Medical Association and, 19–20,
        22
    as an aspect of mental health, 29, 36, 177,
        181
    as chief complaint, 39
    organizational health assessment and, 187,
        191
    process of, 80–81
    in 4Ps Model of Strategic Transformation,
        15, 17
Power
    of caring, 75
    of positive emotions, 72–74
    of positive thinking, 63
    of rewards, 136–137
*The Power of Focus* (Canfield, Hansen, Hewitt),
    154
*The Power of Positive Thinking* (Peale), 63
Price, Colin, 40
Priest, Geoffrey, 102
*Primal Leadership* (Goleman), 31, 37, 75
Prioritization, of goals and objectives, 116–117,
    122, 167
Productivity, 30, 38, 65
Progress, assessment of, 119, 122
Purdy, Roger, 172
Purpose
    American Medical Association and, 20– 21
    as an aspect of spiritual realm, 29
    of Apple, 24
    of Berkshire Hathaway, Code of Business
        Conduct and Ethics, 52
    of California Medical Association, 169
    core, 46–49
    in 5Ps summit, 161–162
    Netflix story and, 48–49
    organizational health assessment and, 189,
        192–193
    prescription, 58–59
    in 4Ps Model of Strategic Transformation,
        14
    San Francisco Medical Society, 47–48
    sense of, organizations and, 37

**Q**
Quality of execution, healthy organization and,
    40

**R**
Rapport
    building, 94–98, 128
    creating buy-in to vision and, 91

Reality check, 116, 122, 165
Renewal
    as element of perseverance, 145, 147–149
    in 5Ps summit, 168
    improving, 155
    leaders and, 33
    organizations and, 33, 40
Resources, 115–116, 165, 167
Rewards, 119–120, 131, 136–137
Right-brain thinking, 83–84, 89
Robbins, Tony, 97
Root cause analysis, 40
Rossman, Martin, 83, 85
Rovetti, Kathie, 97
Russell Reynolds, 117

**S**
San Francisco Medical Society (SFMS), mission
    statement of, 47–48
*Saturday Review,* 74
Scott, Robert, 144
Sculley, John, 151
Self-leadership tips, 30
Self-management, 31
*Servant Leadership* (Greenleaf), 32
Service to others, 32
*7 Habits of Highly Effective People* (Covey), 33,
    91, 109, 148
7 Habits trainer (workshop), 55
*The Seven Spiritual Laws of Success* (Chopra),
    117
SFMS. *See* San Francisco Medical Society
    (SFMS)
SMART Goals method, 107, 110
Speech coach, seeking help from, 103
Speech patterns, communicators and, 98
Spencer Stuart, 124
Spiritual aspect
    of an organization, 15–16
    of leadership, 32
    of organizational health, 36
    of personal health, 29
Strategic plan, 158. *See also* Strategic plan
    development
    healthy organizations and, 37
    time frame and, 150
Strategic plan development
    building teams, 115
    creating feedback loop to assess progress,
        119
    creating timeline, 110–111, 113
    determining resources, 115–116
    developing goals and objectives, 109–110,
        112, 116–117
    doing reality check, 116

internal and external organizational
    analysis, 106
open to new opportunities, 117–118
personal strategic planning, 120–122
rewarding teams, 119–120
telling others about goals, 118
working-backwards process, 108–109, 112,
    114
Strategic transformation 4Ps Model. *See also*
    Strategic transformation summit
    building dynamic organization, 17
    defining 4Ps of organizational
        transformation, 14–16
    diagnosing and treating, 25–26
    diagnosing organizations from outside-in,
        17–18
    4Ps for organizational transformation, 20–23
    looking within an organization, 19–20
    success of Apple, 23–24
Strategic transformation summit
    California Medical Association, 169–172
    pre-summit preparation, 159–169
    putting all 5 Ps together, 158–159
    transforming the organization, 172–173
Stress, 30–31, 33–34
Successories, 63, 145
*Survivor* (TV show), 136–137
SWOT analysis, 106, 109, 121, 160, 164
*Synchronicity: The Inner Path of Leadership*
    (Jaworski), 32


T
Team building, 115, 132–134
Teams, rewarding, 119–120
"The C.E.O in Politics" (Brooks), 143
Thinking, 63, 83–84, 89
Thompson, Steve, 170
360-degree assessments/personality testing, 39
Time, 50, 68, 108, 110, 165
*Time Magazine,* 23
TJC. *See* The Joint Commission (TJC)
"To Err is Human" (Institute of Medicine),
    135
*Toy Story* (film), 151
*Transitions* (Bridges), 70
Turngren, Robert, 102


U
UCLA Anderson School of Management, 81,
    113


V
Values, core. *See* Core Values
Vision, 37, 111
    building rapport, 94–96, 103
    connecting with your audience, 90–91
    creating and communicating, 102–103
    creative problem solving and, 89–90
    in 5Ps summit, 163–164
    Guided Imagery Exercise, 86–89
    importance in an organization, 81–83
    leading with, 101–103
    listening and, 91–94
    Neuro-Linguistic Programming (NLP),
        96–101
    organizational, creating, 85–86
    start of, 83–84
Visionary, as leadership style, 75
Vision statement, 46
Visual communicators, 98–101
Visualization tool, 85
Void, as phase 2 of transition, 71


W
Wall Street Debacle, 51–52
*Wall Street Journal,* 151
Walters, Barbara, 52
*Whose Line is it Anyway?* (TV show), 73, 75
*Wired,* 124
Work ethics, of Generation Y, 131
Working-backwards
    diagram, 114
    process, 108–109
    to set goals, 112
Workplace
    biochemistry of emotions, 65–66
    negative emotions effect, 64–65
    passion, 75–78
    positive attitude effect, 62–64
    power of caring, 75
    power of positive emotions, 72–74
    recognizing burnout, 72
    releasing negative emotions, 66–72
Wozniak, Steve, 150


Y
Yerkes-Dodson Law, 30


Z
Zappos, 52–53, 124